BASIC TRAINING FOR SPIRITUAL COMBAT

Jay has written a fun book to read with a powerful message.

NEIL ANDERSON

AUTHOR, *VICTORY OVER THE DARKNESS* AND *THE BONDAGE BREAKER*
FOUNDER, FREEDOM IN CHRIST MINISTRIES

In 1992, I was a 37-year-old Navy SEAL and former Marine, living in Leavenworth, Kansas, and attending the U.S. Army Command and General Staff College. While there, I attended a conference at the base chapel led by Jay Carty, during which he taught the principles in this book. By the time the conference was over, I had accepted Christ's sacrifice for me.

Your spiritual battles as a Christian will be many and varied. Sometimes, you will see the enemy coming afar off and have adequate time to prepare your defense for his assault. At other times, you will be caught in a deadly ambush and may only have a few moments to literally fight for your life. The basic training principles in Jay's book will benefit you greatly in your preparation for spiritual combat as a member of God's army. May you fight well for Jesus' sake.

DAVID T. PITTELKOW

CAPTAIN, UNITED STATES NAVY
TAMPA, FLORIDA

Part of Officers' Christian Fellowship is about ministry
to young people—cadets, midshipmen and high school students.
Although *Basic Training for Spiritual Combat* is for all of us,
I recommend it as a field manual for all young leaders who
will be future officers in the United States military.

BRUCE L. FISTER

LIEUTENANT GENERAL, UNITED STATES AIR FORCE (RET.)
EXECUTIVE DIRECTOR, OFFICERS' CHRISTIAN FELLOWSHIP OF THE USA

Jay Carty has written a practical, tactical and biblically sound field
manual for Christian soldiers in the trenches. He has provided the start
point, the route of march, the checkpoints, the intermediate objectives
and the obstacles to avoid that will lead to spiritual victory. If you are
searching for theory or theology that will provide you with more head
knowledge for Christian living in our postmodern age, you've probably
come to the wrong place. This book is a practical, down-to-earth,
in-your-face, let's-go-to-war kind of book.

DON F. SNOW

LIEUTENANT COLONEL, UNITED STATES ARMY (RET.)
ASSOCIATION FOR CHRISTIAN CONFERENCES TEACHING AND SERVICE, STAFF
REPRESENTATIVE TO ASIA AND THE PACIFIC

JAY CARTY

Regal

From Gospel Light
Ventura, California, U.S.A.

PUBLISHED BY REGAL BOOKS
FROM GOSPEL LIGHT
VENTURA, CALIFORNIA, U.S.A.
PRINTED IN THE U.S.A.

Regal

Regal Books is a ministry of Gospel Light, a Christian publisher dedicated to serving the local church. We believe God's vision for Gospel Light is to provide church leaders with biblical, user-friendly materials that will help them evangelize, disciple and minister to children, youth and families.

It is our prayer that this Regal book will help you discover biblical truth for your own life and help you meet the needs of others. May God richly bless you.

For a free catalog of resources from Regal Books/Gospel Light, please call your Christian supplier or contact us at 1-800-4-GOSPEL *or* www.regalbooks.com.

All Scripture quotations, unless otherwise indicated, are taken from the NEW AMERI-CAN STANDARD BIBLE®, Copyright © 1960, 1962, 1963, 1968, 1971, 1972, 1973, 1975, 1977, 1995 by The Lockman Foundation.

Other versions used are
NLT—Scripture quotations marked *(NLT)* are taken from the *Holy Bible*, New Living Translation, copyright © 1996. Used by permission of Tyndale House Publishers, Inc., Wheaton, Illinois 60189. All rights reserved.
NIV—Scripture taken from the *Holy Bible, New International Version*®. Copyright © 1973, 1978, 1984 by International Bible Society. Used by permission of Zondervan Publishing House. All rights reserved.

Revised Regal edition published 2005.

Library of Congress Cataloging-in-Publication Data

Carty, Jay.
   [Counterattack]
   A one-on-one guide : basic training for spiritual combat / Jay Carty.
      p. cm.
   Originally published: Counterattack. Sisters, Or. : Multnomah Press, c1993.
   ISBN 0-8307-3716-2 (trade pbk.)
   1. Spiritual warfare. I. Title.
   BV4509.5.C383 2005
   248.4—dc22   2004029568

Rights for publishing this book in other languages are contracted by Gospel Light Worldwide, the international nonprofit ministry of Gospel Light. Gospel Light Worldwide also provides publishing and technical assistance to international publishers dedicated to producing Sunday School and Vacation Bible School curricula and books in the languages of the world. For additional information, visit www.gospellightworld-wide.org; write to Gospel Light Worldwide, P.O. Box 3875, Ventura, CA 93006; or send an e-mail to info@gospellightworldwide.org.

DEDICATION

This book is dedicated to Tom White, my friend and the Lord's prayer warrior and servant. Through Tom I learned the reality of spiritual warfare and the value of warfare prayer. Tom taught me how to stand firm and use the sword of the Spirit (the spoken Word) against the enemy. The origins of and concepts behind the prayers in this book are mostly his. Tom White is the founder of Front Line Ministries in Corvallis, Oregon.

CONTENTS

**Part 1: Warfare to Break Footholds of Anger—
Have Your Nostrils Flared Lately?**

**Part 2: Warfare to Break Footholds of Immorality—
Sometimes It's Sin and Sometimes It's Not . . .
or, Will I Burn if I Get the Hots?**

Part 3: Warfare to Break Footholds of Godlessness— Are You Chasing After Wind?

ACKNOWLEDGMENTS

To John Trent, who is one of the few guards who will pass the ball inside. He encouraged me to write, proofed a manuscript and opened the doors to first get me published almost 20 years ago.

PREFACE

Everyone has a trademark. This story is mine. It has nothing to do with the objectives of this book, but it will help you get acquainted with me.

I played for the Los Angeles Lakers the year Wilt Chamberlain was traded from Philadelphia to L.A. (1969). Also on the team were Jerry West, one of the best guards of all time, and Elgin Baylor, one of the best forwards the game has ever produced.

I didn't get to play much. My contribution to the team was to sit (there was never anyone sitting in front of me), drink Gatorade and yell, "Nice rebound"; "Way to hustle"; "Great shot." I was usually bloated by halftime.

The highlight of my career came in Boston Garden against the Celtics, back in the days of Bill Russell and company. Boston had a terrific team.

I was in my usual seat, sipping and leading cheers. It was the start of the second quarter. The coach hollered, "Carty!"

I poured a cup of Gatorade and said to the guy next to me, "Pass this down to the coach. He must be thirsty."

"No," the coach yelled, "I don't want this. Get your warm-ups off. I want you to play."

I was baffled. The game hadn't been decided yet.

He hollered again, "Get your warm-ups off and get in the game!"

Jumping to my feet, I whipped off my lightweight jacket and threw it on the floor. We wore breakaway warm-up pants. (Breakaway warm-ups have snaps down the sides and under the inseam so all you have to do is grab the waistband, give it a yank and you're out of them.)

I grabbed the waistband and started to pull. All of a sudden I had a flashback to a friend of mine who played for the Detroit Pistons. As he started to go into the game, he yanked off his warm-up pants—and all who were watching that televised game saw that all he had on underneath was a "smile"! Can you imagine?

I thought, *Ohhh, I don't want that happenin' to me*, so I took a peek. Relief. I'd remembered my shorts. "All right! I'm ready to go."

By the way, my nickname was "Golden Wheels" because I was so slow. The Laker announcer, Chick Hearn, always said that when I ran it looked like I was treading wood. I had the most rare legs anyone had ever seen. Everybody knew I was slow. I couldn't jump much either. I'm the guy who got the saying going, "There's nothin' quicker than white hang time."

I said, "Coach, what do you want me to do?" The coach was a master strategist. "Carty, you're going to fast-break."

"You're out of your gourd. Nobody would ever expect it. No wonder you're the coach; only a genius would think of a thing like that."

I played back in the days when there was a center jump at the start of the quarter. Wilt usually got the tip from Russell.

In the huddle our coach explained what he wanted us to do. He told me to take off running for their hoop as the referee threw the ball up for the tip-off. Wilt would tap it to Elgin and, without looking, Elgin was to hit the ball back toward their hoop. Since no one would ever expect me to fast-break, I should be able to get the ball and score a layup in Boston Garden.

As I thought about it I realized the coach was right. Havlicek won't expect me to go. When I take off running I'll get a couple of steps head start before he reacts. Then he'll stand and look at me, doing a double take, because he won't remember ever seeing anything working that hard going that slow. That should give me a couple more steps head start.

Now if he gives me three or four steps, that's a quarter of a court for me. With only a quarter of a court to go, surely if he's got an entire half court to go, we should at least get to the hoop at the same time. And if we do, I'm three inches taller.

I should be able to score a layup.

It sounded like a great plan. So I lined up. It was going to be hard to run with my legs shaking. I was nervous, having never played in Boston Garden before.

As the ref tossed the ball, I took off running. Wilt tapped to Elgin and he hit the ball backward, slightly to my side. The plan was working perfectly. There was nothing between the hoop and me. All I had to do was dribble three times and I'd be in.

I'm a forward, not a guard. Guards are better ball handlers than forwards. That's just the way it is. And I'm right-handed, not left. But I would have to dribble with my left-hand because when Havlicek showed, he'd blast from the right side, and you always want to keep your body between the ball and the defensive man. That would be hard for me. To dribble with my left-hand, I mean. But I figured, hey, I'd push it out there in front, run and catch up to it, push it out there again, and run and catch up. Surely I could do that three times.

Havlicek realized he'd been had and sounded like Fred Flintstone driving his car. I could hear his pitter-patter on the hardwood. He was coming after me and I knew he was close, because I could feel his breath on the back of my neck.

As I got to the hoop, I planted my right foot in order to transfer my forward momentum into a stationary position to allow my inertia to carry me skyward. I was going to jump!

Havlicek made a giant mistake. He misjudged my speed. I was going much slower than he thought and he just kind of flashed on by. I soared into the air (at least two or three inches) and placed the ball on the glass, an inch and a half too far over to the right. The ball caught the inside lip of the rim and spun in the cylinder twice. It looked like it might spin out.

I thought, *Please don't miss a layup in Boston Garden on national TV. Please go in, please!*

It did. I was one-for-one. I had two points. I said to myself, *This game's easy.*

The Celtics went down and missed a shot. We got the rebound and came down on offense. Someone threw me the ball, 23-feet out on the left side. I thought, *Hmmm, let's consider the alternatives.* My first option was to pass.

Since I had the ball there were four of my guys to pass to, but they were being guarded by five of theirs. The odds were bad, so I decided not to throw it.

My second option was to dribble. That's where you bounce the ball. But I wear size 15 shoes. That's a lot of irregular surface on the floor. My dad used to say that my feet were the biggest things he ever saw that didn't have guts in them. What happens when a round ball hits an irregular surface? Who knows, so I didn't dare dribble.

Now only 8 seconds were left on the 24-second clock. What do you think I should've done? Yes! Let it go from 23 feet out. So I cranked one off.

As the ball left my hand it was straight, which kind of surprised me. Shots I put up were rarely straight. If the distance was right it would make that sound that is so special to basketball players. You know the sound—"swish." That's the sound the ball makes when it just touches net, having passed through the hoop, not under it. You do understand the difference? Good!

My shot made that wonderful "swish" sound. Now I was two-for-two with four points. I thought, *Bonus. Give the kid a bonus. And don't pull me yet. I'm doing great, let me go some, I'm bordering on awesome!*

The Celtics returned to their end, shot, missed and we rebounded again. As our offense began I was on the right side, 20 feet out. Somebody threw me the ball. Without hesitating, I said, "In your face! I'm going to do it from 20!"

Bingo! Three-for-three—six points. I thought, *Rookie of the year! Get it all while you're here! Don't mess around, just get all there is to get.*

The Celtics went down, shot, missed and we got the rebound. This time somebody else shot. Boy, was I mad! I wanted the ball. Give me that ball! I went in to get the rebound and was standing next to the great Bill Russell.

The shot missed and bounced straight into the air. Russell rocketed to the roof for the rebound. I had never seen anybody jump that high. I couldn't believe it. I turned and stared him right in the navel.

But the ball hit the front of the rim as it came down. Bill hadn't expected that and mistimed his jump. As he started down the ball started down, just above his reach. Using my legs as coiled springs I again soared into the air (two or three inches) and snatched the rebound.

Russell waited for me to shoot. He stood there with his arm extended upward, legs coiled, poised, waiting for my jump shot so he could tattoo "Spalding" across my forehead. But I already had jumped, only he didn't know it. I put the ball up quickly and it went in.

Now I had eight points at Boston Garden, and all of a sudden it happened. To this day I don't know who did it. Somebody had sucked the last bit of oxygen out of the gym.

A person can't run that hard just after consuming that much Gatorade. You'll "cough your cookies" for sure. And that's what I did—on national television. It was the highlight of my career.

CRUCIAL CONCEPTS FOR WAR

I have a friend, Don Snow, who is retired from the Army. He finished his tour in Vietnam and has some great stories. My favorite is about his first night mission.

Upon entering a village one particularly black, inky night, Don heard breathing on the other side of a fence. When he took a step, a step was taken on the other side. When he stopped, it stopped. And so it went, the full length of the fence.

As Don approached the end of the barrier, he slipped the safety on his M-2 carbine and set it on automatic. His heart beat wildly, tension sweat soaked through his shirt, and the pit of his stomach ached with emotion. Each muscle quivered and twitched. He breathed shallow and rapid. The moment was intense. There was no way to know how many enemy Vietcong were on the other side. But Don was ready for whatever might happen. He was a well-trained veteran.

As he got to the end of the fence, he took as deep a breath as he could and held it. He still heard breathing on the other side, but the steps had stopped. Then, with all the strength, quickness and agility he had, my friend coiled and sprang around the comer with his carbine blazing. To his surprise he killed the biggest pig in Vietnam.

The poor hog never knew what hit him. For that matter, the animal didn't even know there was a war going on, and until that moment didn't care. Most people are like that pig. They don't know a literal war is going on, and they don't care.

God's Word talks about war raging in the supernatural heavenlies. There is a battle raging—and we are the objects of the fray. To the winner goes the spoils the old saying goes. Satan wants us and God wants us. The devil wants us because he hates God. God wants us because He loves us. Still, the whole idea of spiritual warfare is hard to grasp.

Whether we realize it or not, each of us also lives in a combat zone. A battle rages on Earth as well as in supernatural dimensions. And whether we like it or not, there are going to be casualties. Casualties are one of the products of war.

Satan's strategy in the war is twofold: (1) to keep non-believers from believing; and (2) to keep believers powerless in sin. He uses lies, accusations and confusion as his primary weapons for occupying the ground he takes from us and for keeping us on the defensive.

However, we do have protective armor and an arsenal of our own. Otherwise it wouldn't be a war. Without our weapons and armor the enemy would walk right over us. But unless we're aware of the battle, we won't have a reason to put on the protection and utilize the arsenal. Only then can we counterattack and take the offensive.

Pigs don't like basic training; they're not aware of the need and quickly become casualties. Soldiers may not like spending time on the basics either, but at least they realize the necessity. Boot camp prepares us for war by teaching us the basics of fighting. That's what this chapter is all about. You may not like it, but it's necessary. Plow through it anyway. Don't be a pig.

We'll be discussing three concepts you need to know before counterattacking the enemy in battle: Éclairs in Your Refrigerator; Polar Bear

Alert; and How Aliens Get Their Feet in the Door. Don't treat these three subjects lightly. Learn about these ideas now to understand what's being said later.

ÉCLAIRS IN YOUR REFRIGERATOR

Why is it most Christians are not empowered by the Holy Spirit most of the time? I believe it's because of what I call "éclairs in your refrigerator."

Picture this. Let's assume you're on a diet, but on the way home you walk by your favorite bakery. The pangs of hunger are overwhelming and at that moment you would rather be fat than hungry, so you go in and buy two chocolate éclairs. Upon arriving home you feel guilty and somewhat defeated so you put the éclairs in the refrigerator and go into the living room where you kneel and pray, "Oh, God, help me not to eat those chocolate éclairs."

How much power was in that prayer? The answer is to be found in the analysis of your heart. Why did you put the éclairs in the refrigerator? To save them, of course. You wanted to make sure the pastries wouldn't spoil until you could justify eating them. In other words, you had already made up your mind to live against your prayers.

You prayed and asked God to help keep you from eating the chocolate éclairs, but you only were waiting for the right opportunity to chow down. You were giving lip service to God; you were double-minded as you prayed.

Double-minded prayers say one thing while meaning another, and you can't get away with that when you're dealing with God. How can there be power in a prayer when you really aren't open to His answer, especially if He says something you don't want to hear: "Don't eat 'em!"? The result of such a prayer is obvious—there is no power!

You must understand the principle of éclairs in your refrigerator in order to win the battle that's ahead. When your heart doesn't match the words of your prayers you are double-minded; you have éclairs in your refrigerator. Éclairs stifle the power of prayer.

Examples of double-minded people abound:

The homemaker who won't miss her soaps during the week but wonders why she is having thoughts about having an affair.

Teenagers who say they just want to "talk" but go out and park to "watch the submarine races," and then are confused when their passion takes them beyond "just talking."

A man who says he wants to quit drinking but continues to go to parties, to walk by the tavern he normally visits or to keep a bottle hidden in his closet.

The family in debt who prays, "God, help us to be responsible with our spending," but continues to go shopping for entertainment.

The student who prays, "God, help me not to cheat on the test today," but then picks his seat next to the smartest person in class.

The person who joins the church prayer chain to stay current with everyone's information.

The teenager who prays, "Oh, Lord, help me not to do drugs tonight," as she goes out the door on her way to a party where she knows drugs will be available.

These people want to continue their behavior more than they want to change. They ask God for power to do what they really don't want to do—a useless endeavor. They have éclairs in their refrigerator. They are double-minded; there is no power in their prayers.

You may be double-minded and not know it. If you have never asked God to show you the éclairs in your refrigerator, it may be that you have some pastries in cold storage and are unaware of it. You need to get rid of them. They are footholds the enemy can use as a base of operations to oppress you.

God looks at the heart; He's not concerned with your words. And since He knows you much better than you know yourself, you can't deceive Him. Sometimes you can fool yourself, but you can never bamboozle God. If you try, you're only storing éclairs in your refrigerator. Since éclairs kill the power of prayer, you can't look for any help from God when your words don't match your heart.

Start getting mentally prepared to deal with the éclairs God shows you. A failure to clean out your refrigerator will defeat the purpose of this book and will spoil the best reason for you reading it. You can't be double-minded and be victorious. *Repentance must be complete.* Otherwise, you're apt to end up a battlefield casualty.

POLAR BEAR ALERT

Before we talk about this second concept, I want to ask you a question. Is temptation sin? Don't respond too quickly. Before you decide, think back to last Sunday in church. You sat there with your Bible open, listening intently to the speaker, when out of the clear blue sky a flock of wild thoughts flew over and some of them circled and landed—you thought about "that."

You know what "that" is. "That" is the tempting thought you had. I don't know what naughty image came to you, but that was the "that" I'm talking about.

I know what "that" is for the guys; I am one. Men generally have tempting thoughts in one or more of four areas: sex, money, glory and "macho" power. Sexual fantasy is the biggie, but money runs a close second. Honor, notoriety and glory take a lot of time too. Dominant, aggressive men also have a macho, defend-the-poor-with-your-imaginary-karate kind of fantasy.

Okay, so you were sitting in church with your Bible open. All of a sudden a flock of wild thoughts came flying overhead, and one circled and landed. Is that sin?

Doing "that" would be a sin, but thinking "that" isn't—yet. Don't feel defeated with the first thought. You have a sin nature, you have to endure direct, frontal assault ("fiery arrows"; see Eph. 6:16) from the enemy and you live in a world system controlled by that same adversary. That's three fronts from which war is waged. Therefore, it shouldn't be surprising that improper images come to mind. The first thought is not sin—but you're close.

When your imagination comes in *conflict with your* will, it's your imagination that usually *prevails*.

If you make the conscious decision to dwell on an impure thought, embellish it and let it run for a while, you just sinned. The Bible says if you look at a woman with lust in your heart, it's the same as having committed adultery with her (see Matt. 5:28). Or if you look at a man with anger in your heart, it's the same as having murdered him (see vv. 21-22). Sinning in your mind is still sin.

Sin is like a pane of glass with a circle drawn on it. Add 10 pie-shaped wedges and call them the Ten Commandments if you want to. Now, take a hammer and try to break your favorite piece of pie. What happens to the pane of glass? It shatters. It's impossible to break just a single piece. When you've broken one, you've broken them all. That's why all sin is the same in God's eyes whether thought or expressed. But sin happens in your mind before it ever gets expressed in your behavior. If you can head off dwelling on tempting thoughts, you've gone a long way toward controlling sin in your life.

Here's the principle with which we're going to work: When your imagination comes in *conflict with your* will, it's your imagination that usually *prevails*.

That means you will most often do a variation of whatever you think about most. Therefore, it's necessary to discipline your thoughts by taking them captive to the obedience of Christ.

Here comes a flock of wild thoughts. Temptation has hit. Now what are you going to do? If you don't have a mechanism to take the thought captive, your imagination will run wild and you will sin. That's why you need to learn how to have a polar bear alert.

Here's how.

Go in the corner and don't think of a white polar bear.

What did you think of? A polar bear, that's right. Not just because you're rebellious. You are, but not just because of that. It's because you didn't have anything else to think about. If all you have to think about is a white polar bear, what are you going to think of? A white polar bear.

This time, let's try it this way. Make the white polar bear cause you to think of a pink elephant. The white polar bear is going to be the catalyst generating the image of a pink elephant in your mind. Ready?

Go in the corner and don't think of a white polar bear. What did you think of? Did you say a pink elephant?

Wrong. First you thought of a white polar bear, and then a pink elephant.

The difference between the second time and the first time is subtle but very important: *The white polar bear didn't stay in your head as long when you had a pink elephant to think about.* That's a crucial concept if we call temptation the white polar bear and the things of God the pink elephant.

If you can sensitize yourself to temptation so that you're aware when it comes, the tempting thought will stay in your mind for a shorter period of time because you put something else in its place. Since you can't think of two things at the same time, and if you practice substitute thinking, you're not going to sin. Temptation will be removed before sin occurs. You will use temptation as a catalyst to make you think of godly things. That's pretty simple. But you'll need some practice to get good at it, especially if it's not something you've done much.

I don't know if you've ever seen an old World War II submarine movie. The sub is on the surface, and as an enemy plane flies overhead, you hear an "Uugga Uugga" sound from a claxon horn and someone screaming into the intercom "Dive! Dive! Dive!" Then the guys scramble down the ladder from the conning tower into the sub and close the hatch just as the water starts coming in. It's an intense moment that grabs your attention.

You want temptation to get your attention. Whenever you have a polar bear alert it will be necessary to have a horn blast in your head. And whenever that occurs make yourself think of 2 Corinthians 10:5 (*you'll need to memorize it*):

> We are destroying speculations and every lofty thing raised up against the knowledge of God, and we are taking every thought captive to the obedience of Christ.

"This is too far out for me," you may be saying. But stop and think for a moment. This idea can work for you. You can use temptation to remind yourself to start reconstructing the verse, and by the time you put 2 Corinthians 10:5 together in your mind, whatever it was that was tempting you will be so far gone it just won't be a problem anymore. You will have done some substitute thinking and you won't have sinned.

My favorite spot is Hume Lake Christian Camp in California. One day, after teaching the polar bear alert concept, I was coming out of chapel following a couple of high school guys. They didn't know I was behind them. As we got to the street a girl wearing shorts shorter than what was appropriate (a little "cheek" was slightly exposed) walked in front of us. As they checked her out, without looking at each other, in unison they shouted "polar bear alert" and hung a left toward the camp store. The concept works!

Use it against improper fantasy.

Use it to displace emotion in order to keep anger from ruling your life.

Use it when you are shopping to keep from lusting after things.

Use it when walking by the refrigerator if you are trying to watch your weight or practicing self-discipline.

Try it. It works.

Remember, when your imagination comes in conflict with your will, it's your imagination that usually prevails. You'll probably end up doing a variation of whatever you think about the most.

As strange as it may seem, this is one of the most practical devices you can use to keep from sinning, which makes learning the technique worth the time. Don't you agree?

HOW ALIENS GET THEIR FEET IN THE DOOR

A person who makes provision for sin opens the way to the influence of Satan. He or she offers a geographical place for the enemy's clout. That is the nature of the word translated "foothold" or "opportunity" in Ephesians 4:27.

When you willingly stick your face into God's face, say "No!" and refuse to repent, it's as if you took a wood-splitting maul (a fat ax) and drove it into your chest, but it didn't break the skin. Instead it left a wedge-like divot—a place for critters to hide. That newly created cavity in your sternum is a foothold. It's the result of ground you gave to the enemy. Chronic sin produces openings for your adversary.

To help you grasp this principle, I'd like you to visualize a tiny *Aliens* kind of character with a strange shaped head, a potbelly, skinny little legs, lizard-like skin and suction cup fingers. You can see the little guy sitting in there, and it was you who made room for him. He's outside, not inside; he doesn't possess you. But he has a place to hide.

Actually, the alien could look like lots of things, and may not even look like anything at all. But he represents an enemy of Christ, and he's under the direction of the devil himself, assigned to the place of opportunity you provided because you didn't take care of your sin properly.

When you finally decided to repent from your long-term sin and claimed 1 John 1:9—"But if we confess our sins to him, he is faithful and just to forgive us and to cleanse us from every wrong" (*NLT*)—the cleansing winds of prayer came, blowing your sin away. Once again you were right with God and filled with the Spirit. But look closely. Do you see the alien's legs blowing in the wind? The little guy is still clutching the edge of the crevice in your chest with his little suction cup fingers. He's not in your life, but he keeps hanging around because the foothold is still there.

We have to remove the foothold, and to do that we must submit to God and resist the devil (see Jas. 4:7). Submitting to God is not the same as resisting the devil. Jesus was in submission to God, but when the devil attacked Him in the wilderness, our Lord tapped into "The" power source and verbally commanded the devil, "Go, Satan!" (Matt. 4:10). In essence, he said, "There is authority in My name." Jesus submitted to God, but He also spoke words of resistance toward the enemy. Folks, that's a two-step process, and Jesus followed it. No, more than that, Jesus *established it.*

King David probably raped Bathsheba, certainly committing adultery, and had a man murdered in an attempt to cover up the king's sin and hide the fact that he got her pregnant. At least nine months passed with David in a nonrepentant state; we know this because David's child was born before God confronted him through the prophet Nathan. In other words, David's sin was long-term and chronic, and chronic sin usually results in footholds.

It's true that after Nathan nailed David with the words, "You are that man," David—the man who knew the forgiving nature of God better than any other man—sat down and wrote the greatest statement of repentance ever chronicled:

Create in me a clean heart, O God. Renew a right spirit within me. Do not banish me from your presence, and don't take your Holy Spirit from me. Restore to me again the joy of your salvation, and make me willing to obey you. Then I will teach your ways to sinners, and they will return to you (Ps. 51:10-13, *NLT*).

David submitted to God; there is no doubt about it. But not before Satan was given an opportunity to influence him.

The bottom line is clear: Chronic, prolonged behavior in one or more of the categories of sin will produce opportunities for the devil to manifest his influence in your *life*.

Chronic, prolonged sin is like Humphrey Bogart dragging his boat through the swamp in the old classic movie *The African Queen*. Katharine Hepburn had to pull off the leeches. It's like Rambo hanging in the sewage pit. He had to pull out his knife and scrape 'em off.

When you're in the slime for a while, leeches attach themselves to your body. If you just fall into the swamp and hop right out, there isn't a problem with the parasites, because there isn't enough time for them to hook up. But when you stay in and go for a swim, you'll pick up some every time. How fast and how many depend on a variety of factors, but eventually the bloodsuckers will attach themselves. When you finally decide to get out of the swamp, even after hosing off, the leeches remain. They are fixed in place, and washing won't make them leave. They must be individually removed.

Sin is the swamp. Leeches are the enemies of Christ. The longer you stay in sin the more opportunity aliens have to attach. And once they are fixed in place, even the hosing down by prayers of confession often won't remove them. Another prayer is helpful—a warfare prayer. And the result will be deliverance without a lot of hassle.

Remember, Satan is not omniscient; he can't read your mind. He's real smart and can make some pretty good guesses as to how you will react in certain situations, but he doesn't know your thoughts. That's why you'll have to get specific and sic Jesus on him. Christ will yell, "Go, Satan!" or its equivalent, which will get rid of the leeches. But you must determine not to go back into the swamp.

Let me add a word to temper your growing concern. I don't want to give you "devilphobia" and cause you to think you give ground to the devil whenever you slide or stumble. You don't have to worry about the postnasal-drip demon or looking for a demon under every rock. There is great protection in the power of God and His faithfulness. He'll always give you time to respond to conviction and to repent. But don't use the swamp for a hot tub; leech-like critters are the consequence.

THE NEXT STEP

Have you ever been angry with another person, God or yourself for a prolonged period of time?

Did you give away your virginity or have sex with your mate prior to marriage?

Has there been something or someone in your life that has had greater importance to you than Christ?

If so, prepare to check yourself for éclairs in your refrigerator and determine to practice polar bear alerts along the way. Then you can confidently go after your aliens and the footholds produced from your sinful past.

This book will take you through the process of submitting to God and resisting the devil in each of the categories of sinful behavior. Up to now the devil's been able to shoot you pretty good, hasn't he? Kind of like the pig.

PULLING IT TOGETHER

1. "Éclairs in your refrigerator" means double-mindedness; your words don't match your heart. Deciding to live against your prayers quenches their energy and renders them useless and ineffective. There is no power in the prayers of the double-minded. Éclairs demonstrate a lack of repentance and prevent the removal of footholds.
2. A "polar bear alert" is a mechanism used to defeat tempta-

tion by helping us take our thoughts and feelings captive to the obedience of Christ. Since sin begins in the mind, polar bear alerts can be helpful in preventing sin and therefore keep footholds from occurring or reoccurring.

3. Prolonged sin creates footholds, which are pockets of protection for the influence of the enemy. Foothold removal often requires both repentance and resistance.

4. Begin now to agree to deal with double-mindedness (removing éclairs). Resolve to start taking thoughts and feelings captive to the obedience of Christ (polar bear alerts). And with a repentant heart determine to come against the power of the devil in Jesus' name to remove the footholds in your life that have resulted from times of prolonged sin in your past (purpose to give your aliens the boot).

PART 1:

WARFARE TO BREAK FOOTHOLDS OF ANGER—HAVE YOUR NOSTRILS FLARED LATELY?

WHAT'S WRONG WITH GETTING MAD?

CHAPTER TWO

Imagine you're at a bullfight. The matador waves a red cape as he tries to enrage the bull. The beast pounds and scratches the ground in intensifying anger. He's ready to charge. As air rushes in and out, his nostrils flare and undulate. The bull is good and mad.

The most feared event in rodeo is the bull ride. The beast rushes out of the chute, whirling and bucking as mucus flies from his nose in torrents. That's one mad bull. *His nostrils have flared.*

The idea of "flared nostrils" is part of the Hebrew word for anger. "His nostrils are flared" is a great visual statement for someone who's angry. The face distorts, the mouth purses, the eyes squint, and sure enough, those nostrils flare. That person's hopping mad.

Think of the last time you got angry. It may have been earlier today. It might have been yesterday. Perhaps it was last Saturday night. Whenever it was, pause and think about the last time you got angry.

Now, reconstruct the situation and your feelings. What emotions did you experience just before you got mad?

If you analyze the progression of your emotions, I'll bet your anger was preceded by hurt, fear, frustration or feelings of injustice. I wouldn't be surprised if you experienced more than one of those feelings. Anger doesn't just happen. It's triggered by some other emotion.

As we'll see, an awareness of the emotion or emotions leading to anger can be helpful in taking anger captive. When we recognize one or more of the four emotions building, we can then make a choice to properly deal with the anger that will probably follow.

PHYSICAL AND EMOTIONAL "OUCHIES"

How do you react to physical and emotional pain? When someone gives me an "ouchie" physically, I get angry, especially if the infliction was intentional or the result of inconsiderate behavior. It's almost a reflex. Some people think reacting in anger is an excuse to fly off the handle. It's not, but then you probably knew that. Although I know it, sometimes I fly off anyway. Do you know what I'm talking about? I thought so.

I was asked to play basketball on a team with some friends in a city league. During one of the games we had a big lead late in the game. One of their players had been a bit rough.

As it turned out, one of my teammates shot and the rough guy slammed a screen into me. My hand, being limp at the wrist at the time, flipped forward, cuffing him on the ear. It was accidental, but he didn't know it. He turned and looked at me with fire in his eyes. His nostrils were definitely flared. I ignored him.

A few moments later, with only seven seconds remaining in the game, we were standing side by side at the free throw line. I said to him, "I'm sorry about the flip on the ear. I hadn't expected such a hard screen. You caught me off guard." He just glared and didn't say a word.

ANGER BELOW THE SURFACE

In basketball when the game is not yet over but has already been decided, players will often use the final seconds to get even. Since fouls won't change the outcome, the latter stages can get pretty rough. I expected this guy to try and get his pound of flesh, so I was hoping the free throw shooter would make the basket. If he missed there would be a rebound opportunity, and my opponent would have a chance to take a cheap shot.

Sure enough the shooter missed and, yep, you guessed it, the guy was all over my back digging in with his elbows.

I was a traveling preacher then, and most of the folks around town knew that. So I reacted like the mighty man of God that I am—I turned and hit the guy. I couldn't believe it. I had actually hit him. His chest was against my back and his elbows had just done their thing on my shoulders as he had come down from his jump, so I buried my left elbow into the pit of his stomach. I heard the air rush out of his mouth as he dropped to his hands and knees on the floor. I pivoted and looked down at him, my right arm cocked and my hand held in a tight fist. My left arm was outstretched and my index finger was inches away from his nose, pointing in his face. He looked up and I taunted him with the words, "Now just take it. Don't get up, don't come at me, don't do nothin', just take it." I sounded like Rocky.

I stopped dead in my tracks when he said, "I suppose you're sorry about that one, too."

I didn't say anything more. I couldn't. I didn't do anything more. I couldn't. His words heaped hot coals on my head. I was undone. I couldn't greet any of the opposition like I usually did when a game was over. I couldn't do any high fives with my teammates. I wasn't happy. There was no joy. The preacher blew it and everybody saw it. Anger does that, or rather, we let it cause us to do things like that.

By the way, when I got home I couldn't get what I'd done out of my mind. An apology was in order, but I had to wait a week until his team played again, because I didn't know his name and couldn't locate him. It was a long week, but I went and we talked it out. I apologized and he forgave me. Although it's no fun to eat crow, it's better than eating your own insides. Crow tastes better than I do.

Anger Almost Always Comes on the Heels of Hurt Feelings

When physically hurt I don't always retaliate, but I usually feel anger. That's the way it is with physical pain. When was the last time you bumped your head or stubbed your toe? Did you get mad at the object you bumped into? Of course you did. See what I mean? It was a senseless, inanimate object, and you got mad at it because you bumped into it. Hey, I'm not on your case. I do the same thing. We may be cute, but we're not very smart.

What's your usual reaction when you're hurt emotionally? Right again—just like when you're physically hurt—you get angry.

Remember when your friend hurt you? Remember when you got dumped on? Remember how you felt after those cutting remarks by your teacher or coach? Remember your feelings when your parents looked at you with that "you're slime" or "you're dumb" look? Sure! First you felt lower than worm sweat and then you got mad.

My parents got a divorce when I was going into junior high school. It's a time in life when maximum change is happening, a time of utmost stress.

When your folks split up and you're in junior high, you think it's the end of the world. Sometimes you even think it's your fault. Although it never is, you often think that way. An alcoholic parent creates a lot of trauma too. There are some very angry teenagers walking around these days.

My mom was an alcoholic. That meant that when a party was held at our house, I would be awakened in the middle of the night by a fight. It almost always happened that way. Even now, when something wakes me in the night, I wake up ready for battle. It also meant that special occasions were always traumatic; my mom was always drunk.

I had to deal with alcoholism in my family from the second grade until well after my wedding. That's a lot of hurt to deal with over the years—and lots of emotional hurt makes for lots of anger.

If You Haven't Handled Anger Properly, You May Have Given the Devil an Opportunity

I led my mom to Christ when she was 64 years old. She had several dry years before the Lord took her home to heaven. God changed her. He restored a lot of lost years in a very short time, but scars aren't easily removed. Anger lingers, and I've had a lot of footholds.

Has it been tough for you? Maybe you've been deeply hurt. Did your spouse leave you for another? Maybe you've been abused physically, or sexually, and have deep emotional scars.

You might not feel loved very much, and you might even feel very much alone. If it's been tough for you, if you've been hurt and if you didn't handle the hurt very well, that hurt may have come out or it may have been stored up inside as anger.

If you "let the sun go down on your anger" (Eph. 4:26), you may have given the devil a foothold.

"YIKES" AND "WHILLIKERS"

Hurt isn't the only feeling that causes anger. Consider these scenes.

You're riding your bike and a car cuts you off. Your eyes dilate and adrenaline shoots through your body (those things happen with fear; the body just does what it's supposed to do). What do you do? Sure, you do what any fine upstanding young Christian would do—you get mad.

During the summer, my dad often took me fishing in the High Sierras. We usually took pack animals and rode horses. The most memorable trip was when I was in the seventh grade. We took my dog along. It was a mistake.

On our way out of the mountains, the trail got progressively narrower as we descended down a canyon on switchbacks. The creek was

400 feet below on our left and the pitch of the canyon was steep. A fall would mean bouncing on rocks clear to the creek, and anyone who fell would become dead meat in a hurry.

We were on a straight stretch about 100 yards long when it happened. There were two unbroken mules in the string. The skinner wanted to use this trip to give them experience on the trail. The two wild mules had been rigged in the middle of the string of animals.

Susie, my dog, was making her way down the mountain on the high side of the trail when she slipped and fell under one of the unbroken mules. Panic ensued. When the one wild mule freaked out, the other one did too, and they both started stampeding down the trail.

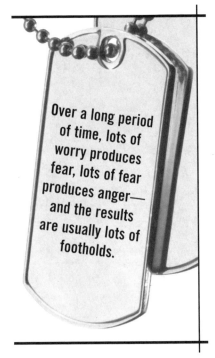

Over a long period of time, lots of worry produces fear, lots of fear produces anger— and the results are usually lots of footholds.

My dad was leading the parade, I was second and the skinner was leading the mules. The runaways pushed down on the two mules in front of them, they all pushed against the skinner, he pushed against me and I pushed against my dad until we were all running on a trail too narrow for passing. To make matters worse, there was a washout 75 yards ahead that required getting off the animals in order to walk across.

Being a tinhorn, I started to slip off the saddle to the left. Remember, that's the downhill side, and it's 400 feet to the creek. I was almost at a right angle to the horse's side when the skinner, on the narrow trail, wedged his horse next to mine and pushed me back up on the saddle.

Miraculously, the string rope broke and the mules turned and went back up the trail. It all happened 10 feet before the washout. We weren't hurt and neither was Susie, but we got a good scare. My dad had been scared the most.

What's the emotion usually following fear? Anger, almost every time.

I thought Dad was going to kill something. He had seen me falling off my horse and there wasn't anything he could do. When it was over he was mad at my dog for falling under the mule, he was mad at me for almost falling off my horse, he was mad at the mules for being stupid, he was mad at the mule skinner for bringing stupid mules and I think he was even mad at the fish for swimming in the creek. Fear does that. Are you fearful about some things? Have you ever asked yourself:

What are people saying or thinking about me?

What's going to happen this weekend? What if I don't make the team?

What if I don't have enough money to make the house payment?

What if that special person doesn't think I'm special?

What will happen if I get fired?

What if he leaves me?

Those are all worrisome things and each is valid and important. Some of them may lead to fear, and by now you know what fear produces. You got it right again, anger! *Over a long period of time, lots of worry produces fear, lots of fear produces anger—and the results are usually lots of footholds.*

WHAT KIND OF "BLEEP" IS THIS?

Frustration also brings on anger. I discovered this playing basketball in a church league.

Although I received Christ when I was 14 years old, I didn't really sell out to Jesus until I was 29. Jesus Christ was, is and always will be Lord, regardless of how we feel about Him. But I made the decision to bring my will into alignment with His Lordship at 29. I wanted to say yes to God in all areas of my life. I still do.

It had only been a week or so since I had made that milestone commitment regarding the Lordship of Christ. We had started attending a large church in Santa Ana, California.

A fellow came up to us after a morning service and asked me to play basketball for the church team. I said yes. I sure didn't want to say no to God so soon. We had one player who almost made the Biola team, four guys who had played in high school, the youth pastor and me.

You may not know it, but church league basketball is the worst basketball played upon the face of the earth. Remember, I had just finished playing with the Los Angeles Lakers only two years prior, so this wasn't exactly a step up.

Well, we thrashed some people rather badly. One score was 87 to 15. It bordered on unfair. One church even brought in four ringers for one game (guys outside of their church who played in small colleges, who came in only to play for our game). We beat them, too.

Naturally, we won the church league, so that meant we entered the Orange County Industrial League play-offs. (You should know the church league team was traditionally the first to be eliminated.) We won our first game, our second and our third. We made the finals against the El Toro Marines—special services basketball! That means the marines on the team are the best players on the base. The only military thing they have to do is represent their commander by "kicking tater" playing ball. They thought we were going to be the next to fall.

The first half was close. We were one point down. Having made some adjustments at halftime, we gained the lead at the end of the third quarter by 15 points. They had some serious guard problems, and we took advantage of their weakness.

One of their players slipped in some sweat on the floor and fell. As he was sitting there, the ball rebounded into his lap. I dove for him, hoping for a jump ball, but I slipped too. While falling I reached out and drove my hand into the ball, completely stretched out, face down on the floor. When my hand hit the ball, the ball hit his stomach, which forced a lot of air out of his mouth rather quickly. The marine I had hit was highly frustrated. He was losing a game he'd expected to win easily, and now he was rolling around on the floor with the guy who was beating him. To make matters worse, the referees were slow calling a jump ball, so we stayed on the floor getting more and more frustrated. He was trying to get loose. I was trying to hold on because I was flat on my face and wasn't ready to defend myself if it became necessary to do so. It looked like it would soon be necessary.

The situation became more than he could bear. Out of sheer frustration, he reached down with both hands, pulled my hand off the ball and bit me on the wrist.

Now I was hurt as well as frustrated—and you know how I respond to physical pain. I couldn't hit him because he had a hold of my hand. Six hundred church members had come to see the game, but I reached over with my other hand, grabbed and slammed his head on the floor. I jumped to my feet and screamed, "What kind of 'bleep' is this?" shoved my wrist in the ref's face and went after the guy swinging wildly.

Can you believe it? My frustration level had surpassed his. I had gone berserk. The referees had failed to call a jump ball while I was flat on my face, and now I would have to wear his brand on my wrist. It was more than I thought I could bear. What did I do? Yep, you pass the test, I got angry.

What happens when people don't live up to our expectations? What happens when they don't come through for us like we expect? What happens to us when we feel we're being treated unfairly or people are taking advantage of us?

Frustration, that's what. And what's right on the heels of frustration? Right again, anger. *People who constantly live in a state of frustration are usually pretty angry—and anyone who is usually angry almost always has footholds.*

IT'S NOT FAIR

Hurt, fear and frustration usually lead to anger. So does injustice. Let me illustrate.

My dad was a Ford and Mercury dealer while I was in high school. The result was that I always had a nice car to drive. At 15-and-a-half years old I got my learner's permit, but I still had to have a licensed driver in the car to be able to drive. You had to be 16 to drive alone. The car was a 1951 Olds, two-door, hardtop. It had been lowered a little, rechromed, painted gold with a white top, with gold and white tuck and roll upholstery, and even pinstriped by Von Dutch. Hey, that was a big deal in those days.

One of my schoolmates lived close by and was already 16, so he rode with me to make it legal. When I turned 16, he told me that all the time we had driven together his license had been revoked because of an accident he'd had. If the police had stopped us, I would have been busted. And I wouldn't have been allowed to drive until I was 17. When the injustice of what he had done sank in, I was enraged. I'd been had. He saw it as a big joke. I saw it as having been taken for a ride, literally.

It's interesting that even though it's been years since I've even thought of the incident, it still stings. I can't believe it. It's hard to deal with being wronged. I've seen the guy since and he's forgotten the whole thing. Not me. I'd been had and something was still there.

What happens when you see someone kicking a poor defenseless little dog? How do you feel when the bully picks on the skinny kid? How do you react when someone has an abortion? What happens inside you when the Lord's name is used in vain?

"Unfair!" "I'm outraged!" "It's not right!" Are those your cries? *What comes on the heels of your perception of an unjustified act? Anger, you bet—and footholds may be the result.*

ANGER OUGHT TO BE GODLY

"Don't sin by letting anger gain control over you. Don't let the sun go down while you are still angry, for anger gives a mighty foothold to the Devil" (Eph. 4:26-27, *NLT*). Did you catch that? Be angry and don't sin. The verse says, "Don't sin while you're angry," meaning, it's easy to mess up when you're mad. But being mad isn't sin. It's okay to be angry, but be careful, you're close to sinning.

We're made in God's image, in His nature. But like God we can make choices; we have a will. He has emotions, and so do we. He gave them to us. What He gave us isn't wrong, but what we do when we're emotional may be. What we do when we're angry determines whether our anger produces sin. Anger is a symptom; it is not a sin. It's possible to "be angry and sin not."

Sometimes it is sin if we don't get mad. According to the Bible, we're supposed to hate sin. "You who love the LORD, hate evil!" (Ps. 97:10, NLT).

All sin wrongs God; it hurts Him. When we understand that sin is the result of our rebellion against a holy God, we ought to see the wrong of it. It's just not right, and we ought to be motivated to do something about it, which brings us to another principle: God gave us the capacity to experience hurt, fear, frustration and injustice as mechanisms to produce anger so we would be motivated to action.

Recognizing wrongs against God ought to stir us up, and our anger ought to motivate us to action. We ought to do something about God being wronged, both in our lives and in the world.

Jesus got mad when God was wronged. He was hurt knowing how much the Pharisees were loved by the Father, frustrated by their hardness of heart, fearful for those they would infect and incensed by their prideful arrogance before God. Our Lord got good and mad. It was the same way when He cleaned house in the Temple (see Matt. 21:12-13).

However, we have a sin nature, and that makes getting angry dangerous. Although anger is not a sin, it sure is easy to sin while you're mad.

Have you ever had an adult put your son or daughter in an unfair situation? Me too. This story is about one of those times.

Referees are my downfall. When my son was playing high school basketball, he was 6'10" tall. He was the Oregon State player of the year and was a Converse All-American his senior year. But since John was bigger, faster and stronger, the men-in-pinstripes allowed opposing players great liberties trying to defend him. Many a night my son came home with bruise marks tattooed on his arms and torso. It wasn't fair, and my anger drove me to action. During one of the games I went nuts. Yes, including yelling, screaming, stomping and questioning the heritage of the "zebras." My testimony has been somewhat jeopardized in our state capitol. Anger drove me to action. The problem was that my action was sin.

Jesus didn't get mad when He was wronged. But then, He didn't have a sin nature. We've got one, and prideful responses are the result when we're wronged, including anger. But that's not always sin. Many times Jesus' disciples gave the wrong answers or reacted the wrong way, but our Lord didn't call it sin. Doing something Jesus wouldn't do may be inappropriate, but that doesn't make it sin. Although it's better to not let the big four—hurt, fear, frustration or injustice—bring on personal anger, it's not sin if they do.

We have talked about four emotions that usually serve as forerunners to what I've generically called anger. Just as there is a progression leading up to anger, anger also has a progression of its own. It begins with a root of bitterness.

THE PROGRESSION OF ANGER

"Let all *bitterness* and *wrath* and *anger* and *clamor* and *slander* be put away from you, along with all *malice*" (Eph. 4:31, emphasis added). The emotions mentioned in this passage are progressive in their effect; each leads to another, more intense, emotion.

Bitterness (called a "root of bitterness" in Hebrews 12:15) is an unwillingness to forgive. It is the seed of a progressive escalation of emotion.

If you don't resolve bitterness it leads to wrath. In the Greek, "wrath" means "hot coals." It takes a long time to heat coals, and it takes a long time for them to cool. However, the coals don't get hot if you aren't bitter.

What comes after hot coals? Anger. The Greek word for "anger" means "striking a match" or "flare-ups." But you don't get flare-ups if you don't already have hot coals, and you don't get hot coals unless you have a root of bitterness.

What's next? Clamor. That's shouting. Then comes slander, which means "I want to hurt you with my mouth."

The last, malice, means "I just want to hurt you." As you can see, big trouble results from an unforgiving spirit. However, choosing to forgive stops the whole progression.

Since most of us are inexperienced at recognizing what's happening, we usually fail to realize we're getting mad until we already are. Therefore, it's a good idea to know what to do when we get angry so we don't sin and allow a root of bitterness to develop.

WHEN IS IT SIN?

When I go "Kapow!" I know I'm mad, but most of the time I'm not aware that I'm getting angry until I already am.

I tend to vent the frustrations of the day on my family when I get home. It's after I make them mad that I realize how mad I am.

Anger doesn't reveal itself to me until I get a blinding headache or until my stomach starts acting up.

Like most individuals, these three people fail to recognize their building anger until it is full-blown. As a result, they hurt someone else or themselves—and that makes their reaction sin. There's a principle here: Anger becomes sin when an unforgiving spirit takes root. It's then that someone gets hurt, including the person with the root of bitterness.

Bitterness is subtle and sneaky. It's like having termites in your house. By the time you know they're there, severe damage has already been done. Almost 20 years ago a friend pointed out my termites of bitterness.

TERMITES OF BITTERNESS

Mary, my wife, and I had driven from Corvallis to spend two days and a night in Seattle with our friends, Dave and Joanne Sundquist. On the afternoon of the last day, the gals went out shopping leaving the guys to sit down over a soda.

Dave looked at me and said, "Jay, I think God's got a chance of using you, but you better get your marriage together."

"What?" I blurted, as I choked on my drink. "What in the world are you talking about? I've got a good marriage."

Dave smiled and cut deeply as he replied, "In the days of D's and F's, a B looks pretty good."

My stance was defensive. "What are you talking about?" I was rigid. "Mary and I have worked with almost 200 college people, and many of them have patterned their marriages after ours. We have a good marriage."

"Jay, I've seen you talk to your wife. You speak to her in harsh tones . . . no, even embittered tones sometimes. You don't speak to a person that way unless you have a root of bitterness toward them (Colossians 3 talks about that being true). Do you have any unfulfilled expectations in your marriage? Have you made any compromises you resent having made?"

I'd been married about 18 years at the time, so I said, "Sure. Yes, I've made some compromises. Of course I have some unfulfilled expectations. *Shangri-La* was in a book. It's not real, so back off a little. We're doing fine."

"Perhaps, but you resent having made the compromises and you're mad about your expectations remaining unfulfilled. Jay, for God to do a significant work in your life, you must desire an A and be willing to pay a price to get it. You have to find out what it means to be a 'crucified husband.' You know, learn to die for your wife as Christ died for the Church. I think it starts with forgiveness. It's the only solution to bitterness."

My friend got in my face and said, "Carty, you've got a problem, isn't that true?"

"Yeah, it's true. I do get upset easily; there must be a problem. Things are pretty good between us, but they're not quite the way I envisioned. Things aren't the way she envisioned either. And to be completely honest, sometimes things aren't 'pretty good.'"

That evening Mary and I were riding home together from Seattle, so I laid it on her. "Honey, Dave and I were talking about our relationship, yours and mine." I went on to tell her about all he had said. I told her I'd decided to try to figure out what it meant to be a "crucified husband." I wanted to attempt to learn what it meant to die for her as Christ died for the Church.

Do you know what I thought would happen? I thought she'd say, "Oh honey, that's so wonderful." And I figured she would shower me with kisses and other gestures of gratitude. I also assumed there would be a payoff when we got home—as a part of gratitude, you understand.

Guess what? She said, "Show me! I'm tired of all the talk. Show me."

Now, my primary reason for saying those things was gone, right? There would be no payoff. I was left with doing this simply because it was right before God and for no other reason.

If you ever decide to forgive somebody, words are usually cheap. Too often that's a manipulative move. But that's what I was trying to do; I was trying to manipulate Mary's behavior. Instead, I needed to follow through in action. Now I was left with following through with my decision for only one reason: it was right before God.

An interesting thing happened in about four weeks. Maybe five. Half of my unfulfilled expectations were met in various areas of our lives together. How about the other half? Well, God showed me they were wrong, and I began the process of tossing them.

If you have allowed a root of bitterness to creep into your life over the months or years, you can bet the progression has started and is probably evident in your life. If that's true, you have traded the power of the Spirit of God for the emptiness of resentment. In the process you have probably provided a foothold for the enemies of Christ. A foxhole for the devil now exists and you can be sure he'll take advantage of every opportunity to devour you.

If bitterness exists, it's going to come out. In the next chapter, we'll look at three unacceptable ways to demonstrate anger.* We'll also study one correct way to deal with anger by learning a lesson from Moses.

PULLING IT TOGETHER

1. The emotion preceding your last bout with anger was probably hurt, fear, frustration and/or injustice. That's why you need to recognize the emotion leading to anger so you can have a "polar bear alert" and take your rising anger captive to the obedience of Christ. People who have failed to recognize anger when it's coming end up being angry more frequently—and those folks usually have footholds in their lives.

2. Anger is a God-given emotion intended as a mechanism to cause us to take action against unrighteousness. It is not sin. It's okay to get mad when an offense toward God has been committed. As a matter of fact, we're supposed to. However, we usually get mad at offenses committed against us. Although it's okay to get mad when we've been offended, it's not advisable; and it's dangerous because we're more apt to sin when we're mad.

* From this point on any reference to the word "anger" will be used in the generic sense, not in the specific usage of the word meaning "flare-ups." Use of the words "anger," "bitterness" and "root of bitterness" will be synonyms and incorporate the whole anger progression.

HOW MAD ARE YOU?

Bitterness usually shows up in one of three ways. Think about the last time you were angry. When were you last "upsetted off?" Did you go ahead and express it? Did you just let 'er rip?

In a group setting I'll ask those who openly express their anger to raise their hands, since their friends all know who they are anyhow. Hands go straight up, unashamedly. They know who they are. You know, too, if you're an expresser.

Are you a suppressor? Let me explain. The dad goes to work, and the boss makes him mad. Since it's dangerous to get overtly mad at the boss (the dad might lose his job), he hangs on to his anger all day long. After driving home in the car, as he turns into the driveway, he sees the bike in his path. His son failed to put it away again.

It's raining, so the dad gets out of the car to kick the bike out of the way. Since it's wet and slippery, he misses and catches the crossbar with his shin. That doesn't help his disposition much. He gets back into the car, wet and limping, and pulls the car into its parking spot. The wife greets him at the back door with a kiss and a couple of problems of her own. Frankly, limping as he is, he's just not interested and manages only a snarl and a grunt. That makes her mad, but she can't get mad at him, or he'll rip her lips off and shove them up her nose, so she gets mad at the older son. The older son can't get mad at the mom, or the dad will rip his lips off, so he gets mad at the younger sister. It's dangerous for the younger sister to get mad at the brother, or he'll rip her lips off, so she kicks the dog. The dog bites the cat, and the cat runs outside and kills a squirrel, making the squirrel the victim of suppressed anger.

Do you do that? Fess up if you do. Parents do that to their kids a lot. Husbands do it to their wives. Why do we do it? We don't properly vent on the person who is the object of our anger. Instead, we store it up until we can vent on someone who doesn't have the strength to get even. It's chicken-hearted anger, and it's wrong. Do you do it?

If you're not an expresser or a suppressor, perhaps you are a repressor. Repressors believe that anger is sin. Most Christians are under the same assumption, but if the Bible says, "Be angry, and yet do not sin" (Eph. 4:26), there must be times when anger isn't sin.

When repressors start to get angry their stomachs start to churn. When that happens they say, "Whatever that is down there churning, it's not anger." But when those angry feelings start to come up, they take the little packing rod they carry around with them—the one with the round, throat-sized disc on the end (repressors always carry one)—and shove it down their throat to keep that stuff down there. Since the feelings aren't allowed to come out as anger, they come out as migraine headaches, digestive problems, ulcers, colitis—and zits (well, maybe not zits, but you understand what I mean).

Repressor, is that you? It's interesting: many of you don't even know who you are. You've denied your anger so long. You've spent a lifetime staying out of touch with your feelings, and it's hard to get back in touch with them. Repressor, you've worked so hard at denying your anger because you didn't want to sin. The irony is it probably wasn't sin, except for the way you coped with it.

Expressers and suppressors hurt others, and repressors hurt them-selves—and eventually others. That's not the way God intended you to deal with your anger. Each of those methods is sin.

"Be angry, and yet do not sin," is what the Bible says, which leads us to a principle: God wants your anger confessed.

GET IT OFF YOUR CHEST

Confessing your anger is not the same as confessing your sin. Don't con-fuse the two concepts. Confession of sin is when you right a wrong with God. The kind of confession I'm talking about is discussion with God so you don't blow it. Let me illustrate what I mean both from my life and from the life of Moses.

After five years, it was time to make a job change. I had been direct-ing a Christian conference center in the mountains of southern California around Lake Arrowhead. The big problems at the camp had been solved, and I knew I wasn't a fine-tuner organizationally. The camp needed a true manager for the next step in its history.

I had two job options, but I couldn't decide between them. I was either going with Churches Alive, a church discipling organization, as their Northwest Director, or I was going to be the Team Director for Athletes in Action basketball, a ministry of Campus Crusade for Christ.

I kept vacillating. My kids were saying, "What kind of a day is it, Dad, a Churches Alive day or an A.I.A. day?" Sometimes my indecision varied hourly.

I just couldn't make up my mind; it was really tough. So we went to see Dr. Henry Brandt, a nationally acclaimed Christian counselor. Henry was teaching at a Christian college in the San Diego area and agreed to see me. I needed help, and I hoped he could give it.

San Diego is a three-hour drive from Lake Arrowhead. When Mary and I arrived, Dr. Brandt wasn't there, had forgotten the meeting and showed up a half hour late, freshly shaved and showered. His secretary had called him at the racquetball club. I was a bit upset about waiting after such a long drive.

We took our Taylor/Johnson Temperament Analysis Tests with us. When we went into the office, the good doctor spread the tests, looked at them and asked, "What's the problem?"

I said, "I'm having trouble making a job change and thought you could help us sort out the decision-making process."

"Well, it's easy for me to see what the problem is, Jay," Henry responded. "There's sin in your life."

After a lengthy pause I offered a rather impatient response, "Henry, perhaps you could elaborate just a little bit."

Dr. Brandt spent the next three or four minutes undressing me emotionally. I was sitting there naked in front of him; he could see who I really was, and I knew it. I was upset. Now, you probably wouldn't have known I was mad. My wife knows me, so she knew. Henry knew I was mad, too, because he's a pro.

Henry asked, "What seems to be bothering you, Jay?"

"Nothing!"

"Don't compound the problem by lying about it; tell me what's on your mind."

Hmmm, he wants to fight. Well, he picked the right guy. My Taylor/Johnson scored me 99 percent dominant, 96 percent hostile, strongly expressive and considerably more subjective than objective. In other words, I was a walking time bomb. Apart from the Holy Spirit, I was dangerous.

"You hotshot." I was indignant. "You don't care about me, or you wouldn't have forgotten the appointment. Then you pull this grandstand move by telling me there's sin in my life, pat me on the rear, send me on my way and tell me, 'Hey, you just talked to the great Dr. Henry Brandt.' Well, thank you, but I'm not impressed. I think you're a fraud, and I think you stink."

He disarmed me with a totally emotionless question, "What else seems to be bothering you, Jay?"

There wasn't much fight left in me by this time. It's so hard to fight with someone who won't fight. I said, "Henry, never mind. Just forget about the whole thing." I motioned to Mary for us to leave.

Henry said, "No, no, don't go. Right now, how do you feel down in the pit of your stomach? Would you say the fruit of the Spirit, as defined in Galatians 5:22 and 23, typifies the way you feel—you know, love, joy, peace, patience, kindness, goodness, faithfulness, gentleness and self-control?"

"That answer's easy," I snorted. "None of those qualities typify the way I feel, at least not right now."

He asked, "Then it's safe to conclude you are not filled with the Spirit of God?"

That question means lots of different things to lots of different people. Some people are really asking if you speak in tongues, but that wasn't what Henry was asking. Others are asking if you truly know Jesus as Savior. That wasn't what Henry was asking either. He wanted to know if I was currently experiencing the power of God in my life.

I put on my sarcastic theological facade and replied, "Now, Henry, I know Jesus Christ as Savior. My body is the dwelling place of the Holy Spirit. The Holy Spirit's in there. I've been sealed with the Holy Spirit of promise, I've been baptized into one body and I drink of the same Spirit you do. But if what you're talking about is the essence of Ephesians 5:18—'but be filled with the Spirit'—then I'm not filled. Oh, it's true, the Spirit's in here," as I pointed to my body, "but right now he doesn't have all of me. I'm mad, and I've spent some time dwelling on my anger. As I understand it, until he has 100 percent of me, I'm not filled. If that's what you're talking about, then I'm not filled because none of the qualities you just mentioned are currently evident in my life."

"That's right," he said. "If the qualities aren't there, you can't be filled." He asked again, "You're sure you're not filled?"

"I'm sure," I growled. "Right now I'm not filled; I'm real mad. I mean, I'm really mad at you, and I'm not handling it well. Henry, you may not know it, but your upper lip is in danger of being pulled up over your forehead."

Remember, I ran a Christian camp, and in Christian camping you live on the grounds, and everybody with whom you work lives on the grounds. In other words, you live with the same people you work with. You can't get away from each other, except by going into your living quarters. So when you get one or two fellow workers who irritate you, you're irritated most of the time. That was me for sure.

Do you live with somebody who keeps you ruffled? Do you work with a person who continually unravels the threads of your emotions? Do you have a teacher who perpetually bugs you, or a brother, parent or a child?

Henry responded, "Jay, when you're with someone who irritates you and your stomach is going crazy, when you think about the grumbling for a little while, would you say the fruit of the Spirit as defined in Galatians 5:22 and 23 typifies the way you feel? You know, love, joy, peace, patience, kindness, goodness, faithfulness, gentleness and self-control?"

"No!"

"In times like that, is it safe to conclude you're not filled with the Spirit?"

"Yes!" My frustration level was growing. It was then he asked me the blockbuster question. (Would you ask it of yourself?) He asked gently, in a soft voice that was such a contrast to mine, "Jay, do you feel that way most of the time?"

"Yes."

It was true. Anger was an ongoing problem for me. I guess it started early in my life. Anger is often a problem for people who have had an alcoholic parent and who went through their parent's divorce during early teenage years. I had quit a good job, an executive position. We sold a wonderful home in Corona del Mar, in the Newport Beach area of southern California, with a view of the sun setting behind Catalina Island every night. We had keys to a private beach. I worked four minutes from my house and actually went home for lunch each day. Talk about having it made. We did, but we flicked it all in to go serve God. Then, four-and-a-half years later, I discovered I'd been serving him in the power of my flesh, not in the power of the Spirit. You see, I was mad most of the time.

Does that ring a bell for you? Are you mad most of the time?

I said, "Henry, how bad am I? What am I going to do? I've only spent a lifetime learning to live this way."

"It's like having a splinter in your thumb," Henry responded. "You hurt your thumb a lot because you use it a lot. But if you pull the splinter, the thumb gets well rather quickly."

"Please tell me how."

"Confess it to God."

I was still puzzled. "What are you talking about? How?" I was pleading now.

"Whenever you feel anger, talk to God about it before you sin."

Have a polar bear alert and take your emotions captive to the obedience of Christ. That's the heart of what he said. You might have to do it 20 times the first day, but it may require only 18 the second. As you practice, your confession frequency will continue to decrease. You might go a few days or even a week or so without having to do it. Practice makes perfect when it comes to having polar bear alerts and taking emotions captive.

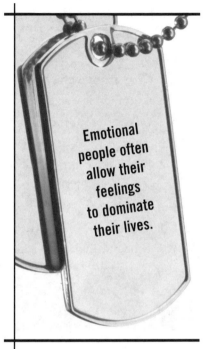

Emotional people often allow their feelings to dominate their lives.

Emotional people often allow their feelings to dominate their lives. Is that you? If you have been governed by your emotions most of your life, it's hard for you to think in terms of taking them captive. After all, emotions have ruled you for years. However, it's possible to begin the process of taking control. Moses showed us how. He gave us a blueprint that works; it's an example of an Old Testament polar bear alert.

MOSES GOT IT OFF HIS CHEST

Numbers 16 tells the story. It's about Moses and his encounter with Korah, Dathan and Abiram, who tried to pull off a takeover in the camp.

They had planned a coup, but Moses didn't respond the way they had planned.

If the chairman of any major corporation had three vice presidents and 250 middle managers rise up against him and try to take over the company, what do you think he would do? He'd probably do some serious head lobbing, wouldn't he? You bet, he'd rip some lips. After all, Mr. Big Shot didn't get where he is being a Caspar Milquetoast, namby-pamby softy.

What if my wife, her mother, her sister and the ladies in her Bible study decided it was time for Mary to take over the household? What if, as I walked in for lunch, Mary, her mother, her sister and the ladies in her Bible study stood, and my wife declared, "Honey, we've decided. I'm taking over. You've been lording your authority over me, so I'm taking over the household." Now that you have a little insight into me, what do you think I'd say? Sure, we'd have a little discussion about lips. Do you know what Moses did when the same thing happened to him? What would you expect a dynamic leader like Moses to do? I would think he'd do some serious Old Testament lip ripping. But when he heard about the coup of Korah, Dathan and Abiram, he demonstrated an unusual leadership style. If you were a follower of Moses and saw what he did, you'd have to think twice as to whether you would follow the guy. Verse four tells us what he did. "He fell on his face."

Can you believe it? He fell on his face! A little pressure and old Moses caved in. He was pushed a little and fell over and kissed the carpet.

How far would you follow a guy like that—a guy who crumbles under pressure? In those days they didn't have the famous bookmaker, Jimmy the Greek, but they did have Jimmy the Jew. When he saw what Moses had done under pressure, Jimmy said, "I'm bookin' this action at seven to five in favor of the rebels." Jimmy thought Moses had folded under the pressure.

Do you know what it means when it says Moses fell on his face? It means Moses prayed. Now don't misunderstand. Moses didn't cry out, "Oh, God, I've got a problem." That's not the way he did it. Rather, Moses prayed, "God, you've got a problem here. How do I fit in?" Notice

Moses wasn't concerned for himself in the situation. His concern was for God and for what the Lord wanted Moses to do next.

Who had placed Moses in authority over the people? Sure, it was God. Therefore, who was the only One who could remove Moses from that position? Right again, only God, and Moses knew it. That's why he knew he didn't have a problem. The people thought they could kick Moses out of office, but they failed to realize who had placed him there. Moses didn't have to campaign, knock on doors, kiss babies or be political to remain in office. It didn't matter how the people voted. Moses had received the only vote he needed. He was God's chosen man for the time. Moses knew all of that, so he didn't worry—not even a little bit.

Moses understood delegated spiritual authority. Remember, one of the ways God speaks to us is through other people, through delegated spiritual authorities. When we rebel against those who have been appointed by God to shape and mold us, we're not really rebelling against the person, we're rebelling against God. Numbers 16:11 makes that crystal clear. Moses eliminated any doubt when he spoke to the crowd: "They don't have a problem with me." And he made it obvious to everyone when he continued by speaking directly to the rebels: "You think you're gathered together today against me, but you're really gathered against the Lord. You don't really have a beef with me; you've got a beef with God."

Dad, do you have a rebellious son or daughter? You need to know that when he or she rebels against you, your child doesn't really have a problem with you. You're the delegated spiritual authority. He or she really has a problem with God.

Wives, do you have a husband who treats you harshly and who is embittered? He's not really mad at you. Oh, he thinks he is, but he's got a problem with God.

How about the boss who is gruff, demanding and demeaning? Where does her problem lie? Yes, with God.

Teenagers, do you have a dad or a mom who provokes you to anger? The Bible says they shouldn't, but if they do, try to remember that they're not mad at you. I know it's easy to think they are, but they're not, they're working through a problem with God.

Do you have a situation like one of those just mentioned? You can pray the way Moses prayed, if you understand who placed you in your present circumstances: "God, you've got a problem here, how do I fit into it?"

Moses knew the people couldn't remove him. God put him there. Therefore, only God could remove him, and he went ahead and prayed in front of all the folks, even though it looked like a sign of weakness. Moses didn't care what they thought. It didn't bother him. He cared about what God thought. Moses also recognized who they were really mad at. With that viewpoint he didn't take their attack personally.

GET THE RIGHT PERSPECTIVE

Did Moses get mad? No, he didn't. *He didn't get angry because his perspective was correct.* He never took their rebellion personally.

You're riding your bike and a car cuts you off. Your eyes dilate and you get a shot of adrenaline. Everything bodily happens like it's supposed to, and then you look in the backseat of the car that almost hit you and see two people doing CPR on a guy. Instantly you realize they're on their way to the hospital. Do you get mad? No. Do you have to pull over and shake for 10 minutes? Yes. Intense fear makes you shake for 10 minutes, but do you get mad? No! Why not? You don't take it personally.

Our perspective determines if hurt, fear, frustration and injustice lead to anger. If you're feeling selfish, you'll take things personally and get mad. If you're not feeling selfish, you won't get mad. If you're close to God, sin will make you righteously angry, and you'll be motivated to do something about the sin with a proper behavior. If you're not close to God, you won't be angered by sin. Yet perceived wrongs against you will easily set you off. *It all depends on how you filter your perception.*

Moses finished talking to Korah and wanted to talk to Dathan and Abiram, but they said, "We're not talking to you anymore, hang it in your ear, Moses, and we're not coming to see you either. We're through taking orders from you. Go bite the wailing wall" (see Num. 16:12-14).

"Then Moses became very angry" (v. 15). What's the difference between verse 4 and verse 15? It's the same rebellion in both places, but in the latter case Moses took personal offense—he got mad. His perspective changed.

However, Moses didn't sin. It's true he became angry, but he confessed to the Lord before he sinned. At first he shouted: "Oh, God, I am so fed up with these turkeys! Lap after lap around Mt. Sinai, they're so rebellious. They won't learn their lessons; they just keep doing the same things. I'm getting so frustrated. If you want to snuff 'em it's okay with me."

As he calmed down he continued: "Oh, God, thank you that I could have this little spiritual 1-to-10 count with you. I'm sure glad I didn't do anything dumb while I was mad. Okay, I'm back with you. You be in control again; what do you want me to do?"

That's the biblical method of dealing with anger. Talk to God about it. Confess it while you're angry so you don't sin. "Be angry, and yet do not sin; do not let the sun go down on your anger" (Eph. 4:26).

If you do not usually confess your anger, if you usually express, suppress or repress it, and have done so for a long time, then you have given undoubtedly the devil opportunities to establish residence. You have footholds of anger.

GET IN THE HABIT OF CONFESSING

Usually, when Mary and I have a fight, she goes into a shell for a week while I do my "Who cares?" routine. One day I mouthed off and started our typical downward emotional spiral. However, that night as we went to bed, I did something atypical. I apologized—without any ulterior motives—and we talked it over.

To my surprise Mary smiled and replied, "You know, Jay, it's been a long time since that has happened to us. Let's use this encounter as a starting point to measure and make sure we keep increasing our time between mess ups."

The sun didn't go down on our anger that night. What would normally have been a defeat was turned into a wonderful victory.

Is that the way you always handle your bouts with your spouse, children, parents, employers, employees, teachers, relatives, friends, referees and God? I didn't think so. You'd better keep reading.

PULLING IT TOGETHER

1. Our failure to process anger biblically will lead to a progression of ever intensifying negative feelings ranging from bitterness to malice. The less intense feelings build into the more intense, but it all starts with a root of bitterness—an unwillingness to forgive.

2. When bitter, some people rant and rave, others take their aggression out on those around them, and still others hold it all in and deny what's going on inside. Anger expression, suppression and repression are not healthy outlets; they hurt others or harm self. But God did give us a way to cope with our anger. He wants us to talk to Him about it—to confess it.

3. Finally, keep in mind that your perspective of a given situation can control your anger. If you see a person as having a problem with God, your response will be far different than if you take it personally. It is possible to be angry and not sin, but it also is possible to not get angry in the first place.

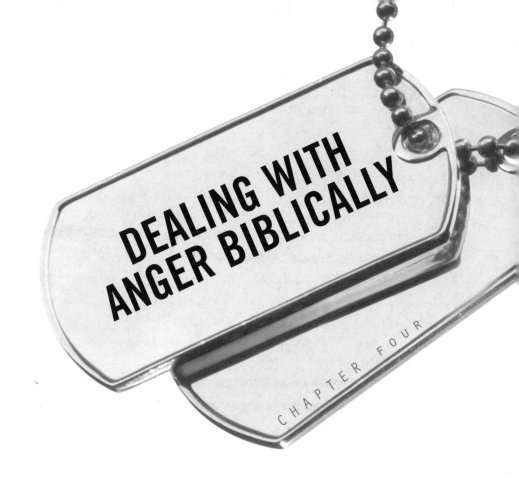

DEALING WITH ANGER BIBLICALLY

Are you mad at someone? Is the twinge still there when you think about past incidents? Maybe you avoid a person because of your feelings. Have you been physically or sexually abused? Perhaps someone you thought was a friend turned on you. Has anyone talked about you behind your back? Are you a victim of your parents' struggle with alcoholism? Has your dad had tough days at work and taken it out on you? Do you have a stepparent who drives you nuts?

Perhaps you're mad at God because of circumstances in your life. He could have fixed the problem but didn't; He let it happen. He didn't stop those things from occurring and you don't understand why. Is your question, "Why me? How could a God of love allow such a thing?" Has "Why, God?" become a statement of demand rather than a plea or a prayer? Have you been questioning more than trusting? Since God is sovereign He could have stopped it; therefore, He's to blame! Is that the way you see it? Do you have a beef with God? Are you mad at Him?

Are you mad at yourself? Perhaps you did something way back when, and you've decided you're never going to forgive yourself. Did you give away your virginity or commit adultery, and do you remain angry with yourself for doing so? Or maybe it was something you didn't do and should have. Did you say some words you regret and, since you can't take them back, have you decided to make yourself pay? Are you *mad at you*?

If you're mad at another person, God or yourself, these questions probably prompted a response. And if you've been mad for a long time, you may have given ground to the devil (see Eph. 4:27). Bitterness is a "Room for Rent" sign on your chest. Aliens are always happy to move in because you have most likely given the devil's agents a place of mooring. Have you become his safe harbor? Did one of Satan's henchmen get tied to your dock?

If you're bitter with someone, angry with God or mad at yourself, and if God shows you that an anger problem exists in your life, you need to (1) forgive so you can be filled with the Holy Spirit; and (2) resist so you can be freed of any footholds. If you do both, you can launch a counterattack.

THE COST OF BITTERNESS AND ANGER

If God reveals harshness in you and you decide not to deal with it, you will grieve the Spirit of God and come short of the grace of God (see Heb. 12:15-17). You actually settle for bitterness instead of the energy of the Holy Spirit. Understand, it's possible to harbor anger, retain it and be filled with the Spirit, but it becomes impossible to sustain it after God reveals the condition to you—unless you are willing to deal with it. It's a principle: You cannot be aware of roots of bitterness and be filled with the Holy Spirit. The two are mutually incompatible.

THE HIGH COST OF HANGING ON

"I'll trade you my bitterness for God's power in you." That's the devil's deal. But it's like selling Boardwalk to someone who owns Park Place. It's a bad trade. Bitterness eats you alive and leaves you battered and bruised. The person who chooses not to forgive will be turned over to tormentors.

The Bible tells the story of a ridiculously rich guy with a slave who had borrowed a huge sum of money. When the rich man asked for his bucks back, the slave groveled, sniveled and whined, so the rich man forgave the entire debt. What a guy!

But there was another man who owed the slave a puny, piddling amount of money. When the slave asked for his bucks back, the man groveled, sniveled and whined, but the slave wouldn't forgive the debt and treated the man harshly. When the rich man heard about the slave's conduct, Mr. Bigbucks turned the slave over to the tormentors, the jailers (see Matt. 18:23-34).

In those days it was possible to ransom people out of jail. The jailers tortured the inmates, knowing the prisoner's loved ones would raise the ransom faster. It was an effective way for the jailers to make a few dollars on the side.

When we refuse to forgive, we are turned over to the tormentors. The torture of our anger eats us alive. The carcass we eat at the banquet table of anger is our own. The abundant life escapes us; peace and joy hide. Sure, we're still saved, eternity has been guaranteed through Christ, but living here and now becomes miserable. That's the way life is without the power of the Holy Spirit, but that's only half the cost.

The other half of the penalty for hanging on to anger is a foothold given to the devil. Remember the splitting wedge in the chest and the aliens sitting in there? Those aliens have a direct pipeline to their boss, the devil. They take their orders from the headman himself. Since Satan is committed to your destruction, need I tell you what your aliens have in store for you? Your defeat.

It's one thing to be bombarded with the fiery darts described in Ephesians 6:16 (you have the shield of faith to ward them off), but having a secret agent sitting on your shoulder is more harassment than is necessary to endure, and there's no line of defense for his attack. He has to be removed, but his removal requires a decision to forgive and an offensive maneuver. And guess what? You're about to go on offense.

This is war, so you'll be using a warfare prayer right after you make a decision. I hope it will be a decision to choose to forgive.

BUT I DON'T FEEL LIKE FORGIVING

Maybe you're saying, "Jay, I don't feel like forgiving. I've been hurt badly. I'm angry and I just can't switch gears. I can't forgive because I don't feel like it."

I know. Really. I understand exactly how you feel, and I understand the struggle you're going through right now. Pay close attention. You're close to a breakthrough. You're moments away from a major victory. Hang in there.

You don't have to feel like forgiving in order to forgive, nor do you have to undergo a frontal lobotomy. Feelings don't have anything to do with forgiving. The same faith that saved you is the same faith that can be energized to bring about forgiveness, and then you can have a polar bear alert to bring your emotions into captivity. If you're used to responding to your emotions, the caboose has been pulling the train. But by faith you can exchange your anger for forgiveness. You *can* because feelings don't have anything to do with conscious decisions. We can make real decisions regardless of how we feel at the time. Let me prove it to you.

I feel like having an ice cream cone. But as I walk by the store, since I'm on a diet, I choose not to buy the ice cream. See? My feelings do not dominate my choice. The guy on the freeway cuts me off. I feel like ramming the rear end of his car. I don't. See? I don't have to respond to my feelings. There are numerous times each day when you don't let your feelings have their way. Why then should you let them have their way now?

If you're a person who has allowed your feelings to run unchecked for years, you'll need to practice bringing them captive to the obedience of Christ. It won't happen overnight. It takes awhile to learn to have polar bear alerts on a consistent basis.

For years your enemy, the devil, has energized your feelings with fiery darts. He has stimulated your emotions and paralyzed the Spirit in your life through your bitterness. But I have good news. You do not have to feel like forgiving to forgive. It's a principle: Forgiving is a choice, not a feeling. You don't have to feel like it to do it.

IF FORGIVENESS IS FORGETTING, I'M WHIPPED

You may have been taught that real forgiveness comes when you forget about the incident causing the anger. Don't fall for it. It's hogwash. Your computer brain can't forget anything. You can control how long you think about something, and sometimes how often—that's what a polar bear alert does—but you won't forget the incident.

Forgiving is a choice, not a feeling. You don't have to feel like it to do it.

God forgets because He's God. But He has polar bear alerts too; only God is perfect at taking His thoughts and emotions captive. The Bible says God chooses to remember our sin no more (see Jer. 31:34). In other words, He can remember it if He wants to, but He doesn't want to, so He doesn't. That's a perfect polar bear alert.

I can have fewer rotten thoughts by taking my thoughts captive to the obedience of Christ through substitute thinking. I also can keep my emotions from ruling and dominating my life. I don't have to respond to my feelings.

Now answer this question: Will you ever forget that incident, the one resulting in your root of bitterness? No. You can never forget, but you can forgive because forgiveness is a choice. It's a principle you can count on: I do not have to forget in order to forgive.

FORGIVENESS ISN'T TELLING

Remember, if you choose to forgive someone, don't plan on telling the person. The person will know by your actions. Telling a person you have forgiven him or her is an act of manipulation. If the person who offended you clearly needs to know about your forgiveness to be released from the bondage of the past, then by all means tell the person. However, it is not unusual for the offending party to be unaware of what he or she has done. In those instances don't tell. Just show.

FORGIVENESS ISN'T TRUST

If I loan my car to a friend who drives recklessly and causes an accident, I can forgive him for wrecking my car, but I'd be a fool to loan it to him again. If your stepfather violated you, you can choose to turn the consequences of his sin over to God, but you can avoid having to trust him until he has reestablished his trustworthiness. Forgiveness and trust are two separate issues. Forgiveness can be given in an instant, but trust takes time to establish and even longer to reestablish. Therefore, forgiveness does not mean you have to get into the same situation that resulted in the problem in the first place.

YOU MAY NEED TO ATTEMPT RECONCILIATION

God may want to restore your relationship with someone. According to Matthew 5:23-24, it is impossible to be filled with the Spirit if you refuse to attempt to reconcile with a person you know has a grudge against you. If you sense God is telling you, "I want to restore your relationship with so-and-so," then go. If the person doesn't want to reconcile, that's all right. It's too bad for them, but you can still experience the power of the Spirit of God. "Being filled" is not based on reconciliation; it takes two to do that. All you must have is the willingness to attempt it.

However, if you have committed a sexual sin or entertained progressive thoughts toward immorality, the higher instruction is to flee immorality. Leave that person to God. Don't go try to reconcile with someone toward whom you have sexual weakness.

Finally, don't forget to write today's date of victory in the front of your Bible as a reminder for when the enemy attacks again. He'll be back.

Having done all that, you are ready to pray. We'll thump the devil's rump in the next chapter.

PULLING IT TOGETHER

1. If you've been mad with someone, God or yourself for an extended period of time, and if God has made you aware of it, there has been a grieving of the Holy Spirit of God and a quenching of His power. Not only have you allowed a foothold to be created, you are now open to the torment of your own anger.

2. The removal of the foothold requires a decision to forgive, but you don't have to feel like forgiving to do so. Forgiveness is a decision, a choice energized by the same faith that saved you. If you know Jesus Christ as Savior, you're a believer by faith and therefore have enough faith to forgive. Do you understand what I just said? *If you know Jesus Christ personally, you have enough faith to forgive, and you don't have to feel like doing it to do it.*

3. You don't have to forget to forgive either. As a matter of fact, you can't forget. Knowing that should help you in the forgiving process.

IT'S TIME TO THUMP THE DEVIL'S RUMP—PART 1

It's now shoe leather time. We're down to the nitty-gritty. It's time to do something besides read. Let's counterattack and go on the offensive. We're going to thump the devil's rump.

Don't bypass this chapter: It's the most important part of the section. Even if you don't feel like it (and you probably won't), follow directions, pray the prayers as directed and resist the enemy when told.

Let me make this distinction. You pray to the Father; you do not pray at or against the devil. There are two major dimensions to the warfare process. Prayer is doing business with God. It's calling on Him and His authority and receiving grace. Resistance is asking the Father to come against your foe and speaking the power of Scripture. The result: the enemies of Christ have to take a hike because your "big brother" Jesus is backing you up.

The devil will do everything in his power to keep you from praying and resisting. Take the phone off the hook. You can count on it ringing in the middle of this procedure if you don't. You'll think of lots of reasons not to pray right now. You're probably thinking one already. Don't run the risk of letting him keep you in bondage. You're so close to winning. *Do not skip this prayer.*

ESTABLISHING AUTHORITY

As you pray be aware of what the Word of God has to say about God's power over Satan. It will reinforce your faith and remind your enemy that you realize he is a defeated foe:

> This great dragon—the ancient serpent called the Devil, or Satan, the one deceiving the whole world—was thrown down to the earth with all his angels (Rev. 12:9, *NLT*).

> Because of this, God raised him up to the heights of heaven and gave him a name that is above every other name, so that at the name of Jesus every knee will bow, in heaven and on earth and under the earth, and every tongue will confess that Jesus Christ is Lord, to the glory of God the Father (Phil. 2:9-11, *NLT*).

> When the seventy-two disciples returned, they joyfully reported to him, "Lord, even the demons obey us when we use your name!" "Yes," he told them, "I saw Satan falling from heaven as a flash of lightning! And I have given you authority over all the power of the enemy, and you can walk among snakes and scorpions and crush them. Nothing will injure you. But don't rejoice just because evil spirits obey you; rejoice because your names are registered as citizens of heaven" (Luke 10:17-20, *NLT*).

God made some strong declarations of authority. In 1 John 3:8, He said, "The Son of God appeared for this purpose, to destroy the works of the devil." The authority of Christ cannot be stated any clearer than that.

You can be certain that Christ has authority over all angelic majesties. Demons recognized Jesus and acknowledged His authority over them before He ever opened His mouth (see Matt. 8:28-34). They know He is the boss.

Satan cannot read your mind, nor can his demons. He is not the antithesis of God. Your heavenly Father is omniscient (all knowing), but the devil isn't. The adversary is remarkably smart, and knowing you as he does, he can make intelligent guesses as to your behavioral and emotional responses in given situations. But he cannot read your mind. Therefore, during warfare, pray out loud and resist out loud. Do that now as you launch your first counterattack.

PRAYER

*Father, I approach You in the name of Your Son, Jesus Christ,
whose name is above every name, and I call upon You. I acknowledge
Your sovereign authority and power over all creation, visible and
invisible. I rest fully in the assurance of Your love for me; I claim
and stand on the certainty that I belong to You, redeemed by the
blood of Jesus Christ to cleanse my sin and set me free from
the accusations of Satan. I ask You, Lord, in the authority of Jesus'
name, to remove all enemy hindrance and to clear a pathway for
my prayer. Father, send angels to war against all powers of darkness
assigned to me. Tear down and destroy all schemes and strongholds
set up against my mind, will and emotions. Remove the footholds
of opportunity that were erected as the result of my sinful past.
Lord God, Your power has been fully invested in Jesus Christ,
and I ask that You bring that power against my enemy, the
one who hates You and therefore hates me, who is made in Your
image. Bring the power of the Resurrection, all the power
of the Glorification, all the power of the Ascension and all the
power that rose up Christ to sit at Your right hand against my foe.*

RESIST

In Christ, I stand firm against all enemies of Jesus Christ
sent against me, and I ask the Father to bring them into the light
of judgment of the holy One of Israel. Expose their schemes,
place them under the sovereign power and judgment of the Lord Jesus
Christ, and shatter their influence. Father, command Satan and
all enemies of Jesus Christ under his charge to prepare to leave
me alone. Bring the power of the blood of Jesus Christ against them.
Defeat them in the name of the eternal God, the Father of all glory,
the Son Jesus Christ, and the Spirit of truth and perfect light.

You are now ready to break footholds and take back old ground.

TAKING BACK OLD GROUND

Are you mad at somebody? Ask the Spirit of God about that as you continue in prayer. Ask for names and faces of people toward whom you have a root of bitterness. Perhaps it's someone at school, your spouse, a parent, a relative, a stranger, someone in your church or someone at work.

PRAYER

Father, I want to make Your Word the instruction manual for
my life. I desire to use the Bible as the standard for making my life's
decisions. I intend to do what You say. I understand the importance
of my faith, and I understand the untrustworthy nature of my feelings.
Therefore, I desire to take my thoughts and emotions captive in
obedience to Christ, and I choose to do what's right before You.
Lord, You have forgiven me of all my sin. Help me to
forgive those singular offenses against me by others.

*I desire to understand Your forgiveness so much that I choose
to forgive. I turn the consequences of what was done to me by that
person over to You, Lord God. The discipline or punishment of
the one who offended me is now up to You. I choose to make it
no longer mine, and I claim release from my root of bitterness.*

Are you mad at God? That's a harder issue of anger to deal with, isn't it? To think that you have the audacity to be mad at your creator is difficult to imagine, but are you? Do you harbor a root of bitterness toward your heavenly Father? Have you blamed God for what happened in your past?

It's foolish to be mad at the One who loves you more than anyone else. Have you ever thought what might have happened if God hadn't let so-and-so happen? Well, your gas tank's either half empty or half full; it depends on how you look at it. When you look at a flower, do you see the blossom or the thorns? It depends on your perspective, right?

If you can't trust God, who can you trust? Apart from Him there is only hopelessness. Would you reconcile with Him right now? Would you trust Him? He knows what He's doing regardless of what you think. Besides, you don't know what's right for you; you've proven that by a sinful life. So don't be foolish, reconcile with God.

PRAYER

*Heavenly Father, how foolish I have been holding a grudge
toward You. I'm sorry. And although I don't understand why
things have happened as they have, I will wait for the good promised to
those who believe and who are called according to Your purpose.
My deepest desire is to have a perfect relationship with You. Thank
You for forgiving me for my hostility and for restoring me with gladness.
I praise You in the name of the Lord Jesus Christ.*

Finally, are you mad at yourself for what you've done? Although you may be forgiven in Christ, have you chosen not to let it go? Is that you? Do you harbor a root of bitterness toward yourself?

In a way not forgiving yourself is like putting Christ back up on the cross. Have you ever thought about that? You keep making Him die over and over again. How many times does He have to crawl back up there for you? The Bible says Christ died once for all sin. But in a manner of speaking, your failure to accept His forgiveness forces Him to keep making return trips.

If Jesus Christ took your entire penalty, why in the world would you keep penalizing yourself? It's just dumb.

Dear friend, let me challenge you: Don't do it anymore. It shows spiritual immaturity; it's foolish. What a waste of energy! Accept Christ's total forgiveness.

PRAYER

Almighty God, I come to You asking for the grace to forgive myself for all I've done. I know You have forgiven me and now I want to forgive myself. Our fellowship has been jeopardized because of my bitterness toward myself, and I want victory over it. Right now, Lord Jesus, I choose to forgive myself and to be reconciled with You. Fill me with Your Holy Spirit.

If you forgave someone, reconciled with God or forgave yourself, take your Bible and write today's date on the inside cover and briefly note what you've done to remind yourself of what to do the next time the enemy tries to harass you. For example:

I have enough faith to be saved, so I know I have enough faith to forgive. Therefore, on (insert today's date), I choose to forgive.

In the future, when the devil brings a memory to mind and says, "See, you didn't really forgive," have a polar bear alert and say, "Oh, yes I did, on such-and-such date. Get thee behind me, Satan; I know what you're about. Be gone. It is written: Christ has authority over you."

Continue to take back the ground you once gave to the enemy.

PRAYER

Father, thank You for taking back the ground I gave to the devil. I come to You now as my deliverer from Satan's kingdom of darkness and his dominion of bondage with all its miseries. I claim the promise of Your Word that whoever calls on the name of the Lord shall be delivered and set free. I call upon You now. For the victory I give You honor, praise and thanksgiving. You are a faithful, amazingly awesome God. I am so grateful for what You have done for me today. I am free, and I praise Your holy name. I thank You in Jesus' name, amen.

PART 2

WARFARE TO BREAK FOOTHOLDS OF IMMORALITY— SOMETIMES IT'S SIN AND SOMETIMES IT'S NOT . . . OR, WILL I BURN IF I GET THE HOTS?

WHEN DOES FOOLING AROUND BECOME SIN?

I will never forget my first week running a camp for junior highers from southern California. During the first three days we found a fifth of vodka, four joints of marijuana and a bottle of downers, and we caught one couple having sex in the bushes. Welcome to the world of Christian camping, good-bye rose-colored glasses.

A few years later I was speaking at a junior high summer camp and did my "Hots" message. One girl had come intending to lose her virginity and had lined up an "appointment" with a high school boy at an adjacent camp. After my talk she followed through with her plan. Later God used the message to both convict and frighten her. She came to us, said she was sorry and wanted us to fix things. How young, naive and foolish she was. My failure to communicate the value of virginity frustrated me.

Most of us don't realize the amount of sexual activity among young teens. Statistics demonstrate that the problem of immorality is widespread among junior high and high school aged people. Immorality is a problem for young people, but it gets worse as they get older.

I was talking at a family conference with a noted pastor and author who has since lost his pastorate due to moral failure. He said that more people have affairs at the age of 50 than at any other age. As we talked I was reminded of my doctoral studies at UCLA in public health. Do you know what constitutes the number one social problem in Sun City, a major retirement community outside of Phoenix, Arizona, and Leisure World, a huge retirement complex in southern California? Get ready for this—infidelity! That's right, unfaithfulness in marriage is the biggest social problem for people in the sunset years of life. How can this be?

By age 65 women outnumber men by a huge number, depending on where they live. The ratio gets higher as they get older. This is what happens. One day one of the men in the condo community is walking down the street. A sweet little old lady sticks her head out her window and begs, "My faucet is dripping badly; can you help me?" Her husband died several years ago, and she doesn't know how to fix faucets.

Desiring to help this elderly damsel in distress, the geriatric gentleman gets his tool box and goes in to fix her faucet. His daddy did raise him right.

After he finishes the job, she says, "Oh, let me thank you. Please stay for a moment and have some tea and cookies."

He wants to be hospitable so he sits and enjoys himself. As a matter of fact, he enjoys himself more than he has in years because she makes him feel like a million bucks. It's been years since he felt this way with his wife. It's been a few years since her husband died and making this guy feel like a million makes her feel great too.

A few days later condo man finds himself thinking, *I wonder if any of her other faucets leak. Maybe I ought to check 'em.*

After a few more tea and cookie sessions and making each other feel like a million bucks, he leaves his wife and home and moves in with her. He doesn't have many years left, and he would like to spend as many of them as he can feeling as good as he can. It's as easy as that—and it happens all the time.

Whether young or old, sex can be a problem for you. *But, Jay,* you might be thinking, *I have this area of my life under control.*

My reply is, "Hogwash," and I don't care how old you are. As a matter of fact, people don't seem to outgrow the problem. Age seems to make it worse. *So, if you are able to read this book, you could use a good sex talk.* It's probably been awhile. And if you are like most people, you have previously messed up in this area. If so, you may have given the enemy a foothold and are under attack, especially if the ground you gave was your virginity.

In addition to breaking footholds, I think it will be helpful to give you the basis for establishing sexual guidelines in relationships and social situations to keep you from messing up—or messing up again. I'll do that by addressing the most often asked question in the Christian world: How far can you go?

Before we get to the meat of this message, you need to grasp three principles about the depth and breadth of sexual sin. The first is the concept of mastery.

WHAT'S THE BOSS OF YOU?

I was babysitting a three-year-old girl for some friends a number of years ago. She was doing something she shouldn't, so I told her to stop. She said, "You're not the boss of me; my daddy is the boss of me." When I told her that her daddy made me the boss until he came back, everything was fine. Even at three she knew that it doesn't work to have two bosses. Is God the boss of you—or is something else?

God spoke on the subject of mastery through the apostle Paul:

All things are lawful for me, but not all things are profitable. All things are lawful for me, but I will not be mastered by anything (1 Cor. 6:12).

Paul didn't say he could do anything he wanted to do and get away with it. He said, "If the Bible says I can't do it, then the matter is settled, I can't do it. But if the Bible doesn't speak to an issue, then I can do it unless what I'm doing takes mastery over me." When something other than God takes mastery, it becomes sin.

God made us to be slaves. We are driven to enslave ourselves. God wired us that way, only He intended for us to enslave ourselves to Him. He implanted this desire so we would be drawn to Him. However, God will not force us to make Him our master. He gave us a will so that we would have a choice. Let me illustrate.

We had a cat. None of us can remember who named her Meow-Face. Our kitty, like all cats, was terribly independent. Sometimes the four of us (Mary, Kim, John and me) were in the family room and the cat would walk in. She'd look for a lap. We'd all start doing our kitty sounds and scratch our legs hoping the noise and movements would attract her. The competition had begun; we all wanted her in our laps. Whoever had the wool crocheted afghan had the inside track, but not always. On those occasions when she chose me, even when my son had the afghan, there was great satisfaction when she hopped up, nuzzled with her head, circled two or three times and plopped. The look of triumph and conquest was all over me. When my gaze met my son's eyes, I'd put my hand in front of my face and say, "Face on you! To the victor goes the kitty." You can't program cats like you can robots. It's really nice when they choose you, assuming you like cats, of course. For some, cats are considered the other white meat, but not in our household.

God doesn't want any robots. He gave us a will so that we can choose to enslave ourselves to Him or to something else. When we hop on the lap of our heavenly Father, we fulfill our purpose in life and bring glory to our God. If we do not choose God as our boss, we cannot avoid becoming enslaved to something else. For some it will be alcohol. For others slavery will take the shape of drug dependence. Workaholics are enslaved to their jobs. Power mongers are slaves to dominance and control. Money is a potent enslaver. All these things and more can form mastery—and mastery is sin. *Anything that takes control of us, other than God, is sin.*

MASTERY AND THE BIGGIES

The apostle Paul continues his discussion of mastery in 1 Corinthians 6 by talking about the two potentially greatest enslavers—food and sex:

> Food is for the stomach and the stomach is for food, but God will do away with both of them. Yet the body is not for immorality, but for the Lord, and the Lord is for the body (v. 13).

You probably know how easy it is to put on weight and how difficult it is to do "pushaways" (push away from the dining table). Most adults suffer from "Dunlop's Disease" (where your stomach "dun lopped" over your belt). It's so easy to let food take over and dominate our lives. The apostle Paul used the issue of mastery by food as an introduction to the potentially broader problem of mastery by sex.

When I'm speaking to a group, at this point I always pull my coat back, rotate to the side and grab my roll of flab over the kidney area that is often called a "love handle." Then I say, "Look at that. It's ugly isn't it?"

Someone usually says, "Amen!" Continuing I'll state my excuse for my spare tire: "A few years ago I broke my leg. Nine months, three casts and a four-inch screw in the ankle later, I gained 14 pounds. In the next two months, I lost 12 of them. The month after that I regained 14 pounds. And they're still there," I'll moan as I point with my right hand at the flab I'm holding in my left hand.

Rolling the flab around in my fingers, I'll whine, "That's not quite sin yet, but it's close—because it's got me. It's got me! *It's got me*!" It gets a good laugh, but it also makes an important point.

Food is tough for most of us. It has a degree of mastery over most of the people in the United States. Obesity is one of America's biggest health problems.

Is food a problem for you? If you read on in 1 Corinthians 6, you'll see that the writer spends half a verse talking about food and seven and a half verses talking about sex. The point Paul's trying to make is this: Compared to sex, for most people, food's a piece of cake.

Paul's first illustration (food) is used to establish the seriousness of the threat of the second (sex). Watch out! Sex can take mastery over your life as very few things can. That's what God is trying to tell you.

SOME BEHAVIORS ARE ALWAYS SIN

In addition to mastery, the concept of sin being both absolute and variable has been woven into 1 Corinthians 6:12. It's necessary to understand this idea before we can answer the question: How far is too far?

Paul wanted to make sure we understood that some behavior is always sin while other behavior may or may not be, depending on the person, where the person is in their walk with God and what the Lord has in store for the individual.

Absolute sins are behaviors that are sin for anybody and everybody. If I pulled out a big gun and blew you away for no good reason, it would be murder. If your best friend did the same thing, it would be murder, too. The Bible says we are not to commit murder, which makes murder sin. It's absolute sin for everybody.

Other examples of absolute sin include stealing, lying and coveting. Although drinking may not be sin for you, be aware that drunkenness is clearly wrong; it, too, is absolute sin.[1] (Teenagers, especially, read the footnote.) The Ten Commandments involve absolutes, which make sexual intercourse with someone other than your spouse an absolute sin; it's one of the 10.

Immorality embraces all forms of sexual sin, including both adultery and fornication. If you are married and have sexual intercourse with somebody other than your spouse, you have committed adultery. The same act is called fornication if you're single. The Bible is crystal clear when it says that both adultery and fornication are absolute sin. There are no ifs, ands or buts about it.

Let me add that the biblical interpretation of murder does not vary according to age, status in life, net worth or background. Neither does adultery or fornication. Being older does not make immorality any less of a sin, nor does being single, divorced or in love.

The worldly terms "responsible adults" or "consenting adults" do not cut any ice with God. Biblically the concept of sexual sin occurring at the point of intercourse is not open to debate or interpretation if you are not married to your partner.

Sexual intercourse with someone who is not your mate is sin, but sin is not always a black-and-white issue. It's clear that some sin is sin for everybody, but it's also true that not all sin is sin for everybody.

SOME BEHAVIORS AREN'T ALWAYS SIN

Every dating person who loves God wants to know when touchy-kissy becomes sin. Parents with kids, teens, singles, the divorced and adults, who are walking on the edge, need to know the answer. Here it is. How far you can go in sexual areas is a variable that will be decided by God, not people, and can only be determined by understanding the concepts of mastery, absolute sin and variable sin.

Let me explain the above statement by first elaborating in some other areas. The Bible doesn't talk much about movies, dancing, swimsuits, cards, alcohol, smoking or television. These and a multitude of other topics are the variable areas of life.

We'll use movies as our first example of variable sin. Some people don't go to movies because they have responded to God's leading or to their parents' decision; movies are a no-no for them. Others can freely go to G-rated movies but can't go to PG-rated shows. Still others can go to PG flicks but not R-rated movies. (By the way, that's me. I do not have the freedom to go to R-rated movies. They are sin for me.) I have a friend who can't go into a theater, but God has given him the freedom to watch movies on his DVD at home. That probably seems hypocritical to you, but it really isn't. It's a good example of how God works with us individually in the variable areas of life.

A person needs to stay close to God in order to hear His voice above the noise of the world. We need to restrict our behavior according to

God's leading. Secular psychologists would say this results from a false sense of conscience. They believe the individual determines morality, not God's Word. The implications of this belief remind me of the fellow who went into the bar and ordered his usual stein of beer. As he was talking to his friend, he felt compelled to pour the container over his friend's head. Afterward he felt incredible guilt and remorse, so he went to his shrink for therapy. After several sessions the man returned to the bar and ordered a stein of beer. The old compulsion prevailed and once again he poured the beer over his friend's head. Upon returning to the psychiatrist, the beer man was filled with joy, because when he drenched his friend, he no longer felt remorse or guilt. He thought he was cured! But he had been cured of guilt. His behavior hadn't changed, and that made the cure a worldly one. If we deny God's leading, we will go the way of the world; therefore, we need to follow this principle: If we listen, God *will tell us* where to restrict our behavior, and He'll make us uncomfortable when we do what we *shouldn't.*

> If we listen, God *will tell us* where to restrict our behavior, and He'll make us uncomfortable when we do what we *shouldn't.*

In other words, situations may change the application of the rules. Let me show you what I mean. I told you God draws the movie line for me at PG; yet, He moves the line at times.

I was the speaker at a high school winter camp where it was a *Jaws* weekend (they were going to show *Jaws* and *Jaws 2*). Since they are older movies and PG-rated, I figured it was okay for me to see them. There I sat watching *Jaws*, sitting with the teenagers I would be preaching to that evening. I wanted to watch it, but all of a sudden the bad language started. After several words of profanity—one fellow on the screen asked God to damn his boat (What if God had? A little bolt of lightning would have left the guy floating in debris, wishing he hadn't prayed that way.)—God used the use of His name in vain to bring my discomfort level beyond my ability to deny His speaking to me.

Listen, I'm no prude. My language before I gave my life to the Lord would probably embarrass you. I have heard it all, and very little shocks me. However, I couldn't sit there knowing I was going to preach to those kids that night. By sitting and doing nothing, I was condoning what was happening in the movie and all that was being said. I had to get up and leave. I told them, "I can't sit here and listen to that and preach to you tonight without being hypocritical. God won't allow me to stay. I gotta go."

Staying would have been sin for me even though the movie was rated PG. Circumstances changed the application of the rules. That makes it important to stay in close touch with your heavenly Father.

God may want to change your sexual behavior. He may want to make your fantasies sin. Perhaps you are too flirtatious. You might be in a relationship that is becoming too hands-on, and God may want to protect you from losing control. Perhaps some magazines or television shows need to be done away with. There may be some areas that have been okay up to now, but now God may make a rule change.

If you're a teenager and it's okay for you to go to PG movies, and you ask someone to go to a PG movie, but you know that's something your friend can't do, then you're asking him or her to sin. You're causing your weaker brother or sister to stumble. Instead of asking your friend to go to a movie he or she shouldn't see, go bowling instead. Don't be a reason for your friend to sin. The world says, "Lighten up, go ahead, you can go. I can go so you should be able to go." Yet the Bible says to restrict your behavior to the level of your weaker brother. God brought this home to me in regard to my drinking shortly after I committed my life to Him.

I used to drink a bit—just a little wine with meals or a cooler on a hot day. My wife and I were working with college people. They're like piranhas; they'll eat you out of house and home. They were in our refrigerator a lot, and whenever the door would open, exposing that bottle of wine, I'd wince.

Finally I said to Mary, "Do you think we ought to get rid of the bottle? Although we only have a little with dinner, some of those kids have problems with this stuff. I think we would be better off not having it in our house."

Mary agreed and we eliminated alcohol from our home. God tightened up our behavior. Having the wine in the refrigerator was not sin up to that point, but leaving it would have been.

God continued to restrict my behavior. I traveled a lot when I was in business. If I was sitting alone in the back of the plane, I always enjoyed having the wine or champagne the airlines served. But if someone was sitting next to me, I declined, since I knew I might be sharing Christ with him or her sometime during the flight. Since I didn't want to confuse the individual, I wouldn't have the wine.

My boss always wanted me to drink with him. I always refused. It wouldn't be a good testimony. "Carty, have a drink with me."

"No, thanks, it's not appropriate."

"Are you still drinking in the back of the plane?"

"Only if I'm alone, never if I'm with someone. I don't want to be hypocritical."

God spoke through my boss when he challenged me, "That sounds hypocritical to me. Either have a drink with me now or stop drinking on the plane." God had just made drinking sin for me; at that moment it became a no-no for old Jay.

You may be thinking my drinking had been sin all along. It wasn't. I was brand new at this whole Christianity deal, and God clearly hadn't dealt with me in that area until the refrigerator incident. He finished the issue with His words spoken through my employer.

Don't start drinking because I used to or keep drinking for the same reason. We can't determine what we can or cannot do on the basis of somebody else's behavior. What may not be sin for someone else may be for you. And what may be sin for you may not be for someone else. Find out from God what your freedoms and restrictions are and remember this principle when relating to others: Don't try to get people to lighten up. That's what the world says to do. Christians are to tighten up to the

.... their weakest brother or sister.

If I hadn't stopped going to R-rated movies, flicks would have mastery over me. If I hadn't removed the wine from the refrigerator, wine would have mastery over me. If I had continued to drink on the plane, alcohol would have mastery over me.

If something takes mastery in your life, my friend, it has just become sin. The point of mastery occurs when something ceases to be a variable and becomes sin for you.

ANSWERING THE QUESTION

Now we can again address the issue: How far is too far?

God has clearly spoken; He just hasn't said the same thing to everybody. *At the point you lose control, mastery has taken over. What had been acceptable has just turned to sin.* If your partner loses control before you do, you just contributed to his or her sin, which in turn made it sin for you. It's as simple as that.

The behavior leading up to immorality is a giant variable. For some the holding of hands may be too stimulating. For others a little kissy-face and huggy-bod may be just fine. "How handsy is too handsy?" is a legitimate question. A high school boy tenderly touching the hand of his date in a demonstration of affection is most likely quite acceptable. However, the married boss who touches the hand of his secretary in the same fashion is way out of bounds. And the people who enjoyed sexual intimacy before their divorce may not be able to kiss their date goodnight for a while. Their desire may be too great and their control too limited.

Although adultery and fornication are absolute sin, immorality most likely occurs before sexual union. However, the specific behavior that actually becomes immorality varies depending on the individual—it falls into the category of variable sin.

What's acceptable? How far is too far?

There is no doubt that intercourse with someone other than your mate is sin. The Bible is clear on that one. It is also clear on the subject of genital sex as well. Whether it is by touch or oral, the result is mastery. Some people say to keep the hands above the waist. Others say to restrict activity to above the neck with hands on the back. What's right for you? You won't find out if down deep you want to be as bad as you can be and still get away with it. You will only find out if you genuinely want to please God. He'll tell you.

God's rules don't change based on time, familiarity or any other variable. Set your boundaries at the beginning of a relationship and don't compromise those confines, no matter what. Don't wait until the heat of passion to figure out what God is telling you. There will be éclairs in your refrigerator at times like that. Voices or feelings telling you to compromise earlier instruction won't be from God. And don't adjust the boundaries after you've been together for a while either. You always want a little bit more. What satisfies at one point fails to satisfy later on. And therein lies the necessity of drawing the lines of variable sin at the beginning of a relationship. Don't make adjustments to God's rules for you on the basis of how you feel later.

VARIABLES IN MARRIAGE

The weaker brother and sister concept comes into play in marriage too. Because of traumatic memories, some sexual techniques and practices may not be mutually agreeable.

What's the rule for deciding what to do? Don't make your partner sin. That rule never changes. Find the things you both like to do. The axiom if both partners want to do it they have the freedom to do it together may not be correct either. Your nature is such that you progressively want more zing and thrill out of your encounters, which can lead to some pretty bizarre and worldly behavior if taken too far. Listen very carefully to God. There may be some things you both like to do that God doesn't want you doing. And it may be that what's okay for one of you may be a variable sin for the other.

Don't be double-minded and start asking the question: "How bad can I be and still be okay?" or the similar question: "How good do I have to be to just be okay?" Those questions are indicators of éclairs in your refrigerator, and you probably sinned when you asked them.

When it comes to sexuality, you oftentimes try to kid yourself. Keep an ear out for God's voice. He will tell you what is variable sin and what is acceptable. And there is another reason to listen carefully to your heavenly Father. He might change the rules in the middle of the game.

DOES THE DEVIL HAVE A FOOTHOLD IN YOUR LIFE?

Does sex have mastery over you?

Did immorality have mastery at one time?

Have you ignored God and participated in behaviors that are okay for others but are sin for you?

Have you tried to coerce people to lighten up while you have been unwilling to tighten up?

Have you listened to your loins instead of the Lord?

If you answered yes to any of the above questions, the devil may have a foothold in your life. And if you are someone who has had intercourse with someone other than your mate, you probably never realized you were offering room and board to aliens. (See the Appendix, "For Couples Who Coupled Too Soon".)

PULLING IT TOGETHER

1. Sex is the biggest enslaver and has the broadest potential for mastery.

2. You will become a slave to something. God wired you that way with the hope you would enslave yourself to Him. However, He allows you to choose your own method(s) of enslavement, all of which are destructive (except enslavement to God). If something that was okay suddenly takes control of you, it has just become sin; it's a demonstration of mastery, and that's a no-no.

3. Absolute sin is nonnegotiable. It is sin for everybody. However, in variable areas, what is sin for one person may not be sin for another. Don't determine what's allowable for you from others.

4. In light of the above concepts, teenagers, singles, the divorced and even marrieds in social situations with people other than their mate should set the boundaries of their relationships at the beginning, not during it. Any revisions in behavior must be made in the power of the Spirit of God, not in the feeling or passion of the moment.

5. How far can you go? God will tell you. You can count on it if you don't have any éclairs in your refrigerator. What you can and cannot do will be established by God, if you will listen to Him.

6. What's allowable today may not be tomorrow, so continue to listen carefully to God. It's important to stay alert for any rule changes God may want to make. Don't forget, He has the prerogative of both lightening up and tightening up. Therefore, you need to stay in close harmony with Him in order to respond quickly to His changes.

Note

1. If you are under age, drinking is absolute sin for you even though it might not be for your parents. Violating the law is sin (unless the law contradicts the Bible), so if you are under age and drinking, you are sinning against God. You may or may not care, but your actions are wrong before the Lord. Going against your parents' words when under their care—unless their commands go against the Word of God—is also sin.

Both the law and the spiritual authorities God puts in your life are excellent sources for God's words. However, we should be like the mighty Bereans who, after hearing what the apostle Paul had told them, checked out what he'd said with the Bible to see if it was true (see Acts 17:11). If you're a teenager, I suggest you do that with your spiritual authorities as well.

THE CONSEQUENCES OF SEXUAL SIN

Beth was a homemaker with two kids—a high school daughter and a junior high son. Her husband, Randy, was a middle-management corporate climber. They went to church together as a family but weren't deeply involved. Actually he went because she wanted them all to go. It was quality time with the kids and they enjoyed eating out together afterward, so he went.

As a couple their mutual interests had grown in different directions over the years. She took the kids to the athletic and school events. Randy usually worked late. There was an athletic club close to the office, so that's where he worked out. Beth played tennis in the mornings with her friends. They called themselves "the girls."

One morning after playing only one set, the game broke up early. Two of the ladies had forgotten a prior commitment. The third left. Beth had a soda and relaxed for a moment at a table. That was when Jack was looking for a partner for mixed doubles.

was a business acquaintance of Randy's and was exceptional-ly nice and "terribly good looking." She played and had a great time. But she politely refused to have a drink with the group after the game.

Two days later she found herself sitting at the same table at almost the same time, hoping to play some more mixed doubles. She had thought a great deal about the wonderful time she'd had. Although it didn't happen on Wednesday, to her inward delight it happened on Friday, and yes, she did have the postgame drink with the group. It seemed right to do so. Jack was considerate beyond words and unbelievably attentive to her needs. It was like he knew what she was thinking ahead of time. He made her feel like a queen, not a housewife.

Staying for a drink was Beth's second compromise. Her first was sitting at the table on Wednesday—hoping. She failed to set her boundaries in concrete ahead of time.

Two weeks later she slept with Jack. She hadn't meant to. It just kind of happened. And now here she was trying to figure out what to do.

Jack wanted to leave his wife for Beth. Beth was attracted to Jack, but he was already on his third marriage. Besides, she loved Randy, even though the thrill was gone. And what about the kids? What was to happen when Randy found out? Where did God fit into all of this?

Stay and be unhappy. Leave and be unhappy. Face the kids and be unhappy. When Randy found out she'd be real unhappy, and so would he. Was it possible to be away from God and be happy? She didn't think so. What a mess, and it was only a matter of time until her house of cards came tumbling down. There would be consequences to Beth's immorality.

God prizes sexual purity more than any other act of obedience, which makes destroying it Satan's number one priority. And since slavery to sex is so captivating, the discipline from God necessary to alter the problem of mastery to sexual enslavement must be greater than any other. It all makes for some very interesting consequences. Beth would find that out soon enough.

SATAN HATES VIRGINS AND PURITY

We live in enemy territory and sometimes Satan is not very subtle. For example, whose name is the only proper name used as a swear word? Sure, Jesus Christ. When is the last time you heard someone in a fit of temper say, "Oh, Jay Carty!"? Never. Have you ever heard anyone miss a putt playing golf and scream, "Billy Graham!"? Me neither. How about "Mother Teresa" when the car won't start? Nope! Listen, Jesus has the most popular name going. No other name comes close. You'll hear it in locker rooms, on the job and in the movies. It's called profanity. The Bible calls it using the Lord's name in vain.

Why is that precious name used as a swear word? And why does God say not to swear? He knew what Satan would do with that name—attempt to pervert it. Even an old jock like me can figure that out.

In the church of Satan, they do everything opposite of Christianity; the goal is to corrupt Christ. The Cross is turned upside down and the arms are broken into a peace sign. They worship a goat instead of the Lamb. Their number one act of worship is the virgin sacrifice. As a matter of fact, you cannot get married in that church unless you've had intercourse.

Satan's desire is to brutalize the virgin birth of Jesus Christ. *Therefore, I believe the number one goal of the devil is to steal your virginity. His next priority is to move you into immorality.* That's what he did with Beth.

Since Satan hates God he wants you to do what God doesn't want you to do. What's important to God is important to the devil—but Satan wants to pervert and debauch it. Why does the enemy want the virginity of our children, and why does he want the rest of us to fall into immorality? Because moral purity is so important to God. To understand its importance, it's necessary to understand something about our sin nature and why God hates sexual sin.

THE IMPORTANCE OF THE VIRGIN BIRTH

When my daughter was a toddler, we had a low-profile stereo that had sliding doors in its top. Kim thought it was fun to slide the doors back and reach in; there was some good stuff in there to play with. There was a switch that clicked, a wheel to spin and an arm to yank on.

In our household a "Daddy no-no" was an automatic, no questions asked, hand slap. One day when Kim had her hand in the stereo, I said, "Kim, that's a Daddy no-no," and I slapped her hand.

Kim screamed but thrust her hand right back into the stereo. I took out her little hand and whapped it a second time. She pulled the same routine. After screaming she thrust her hand back into the stereo. I'm going to make a long story short, but this is absolutely true. I whacked her hand 20 times, and 20 times she put it back into the stereo.

On the twenty-first whack Kim's whole disposition changed. Her whole demeanor altered. She thrust her face toward my face, glared and defiantly thrust her hand back into the stereo while continuing to stare at me. If she could have talked, she would have said, "Bite the wall, Dad! Hang it in your ear, Pop! I'm gonna do what I wanna do, because I wanna do it!"

I couldn't believe it. I was at war with a nine-month-old kid. I'm big, tall and ugly, and I have a deep voice. Listen, I'm intimidating. I can be a scary guy, but that little nine-month-old kid wasn't afraid.

Again I took the little hand out of the stereo and whacked it. She glared, started to thrust her hand back into the stereo, stopped, pondered, folded her arms, exhaled through her nose, turned and made her way to the other side of the room. It was over, but it had been quite a battle.

Here's my point: Where did she get that? I know, from me, right? You bet. *You and I were born with a sin nature, and we got it from our dad.*

"For I was born a sinner—yes, from the moment my mother conceived me" (Ps. 51:5, *NLT*). Augustine thought the verse referred to the sexual act of intercourse. He thought sex was sin. But that's not the meaning at all. The Bible was referring to the transfer of the father's sin nature to the child.

Our sin nature is transmitted through the male. That's why Jesus had to be born of a virgin; otherwise, He would have received the sin nature of His dad. If that had happened He would have had to die for His own sins and wouldn't have qualified to die for ours. In that light the virgin birth becomes a critical doctrine. And now we can begin to grasp why our enemy concentrates so much time and effort on perverting virginity.

GOD HATES IT THE MOST

While it's true that Satan hates sexual purity more than any of God's other mandates, it is also true that God hates sexual sin more than any other sin and considers it to be unique among all the possible sins we can commit. The result is a principle: The consequences for involvement in sexual sin will be the most traumatic and severe God has to offer.

God's methods of dealing with immorality prove my point. He has dished out consequences for it in ways He has never disciplined any other sin. This is illustrated in Luke 17:

> And just as it happened in the days of Noah, so it will be also in the days of the Son of Man (v. 26).

The phrase "the days of the Son of Man" includes the day when Christians are outta here. I call it the day of the great "too-doo." You don't know what a "too-doo" is, so I guess I better tell you.

Have you ever sat in your bathroom, looked over at the paper holder and realized that there is no tissue? All that's left is the little cardboard cylinder. Have you ever taken that little cardboard cylinder, put it to your lips and used it for a trumpet—"too-doo"? Have you ever done that? I thought so. All right, have you ever used it for a telescope? Me too. Aren't we fun?

Well, before our Lord returns there's going to be a very loud shout— "Yahoo!"—and then we'll hear the greatest trumpet blast we've ever heard—"Too-Doo!"

Listen, when we hear those two sounds get ready to leave the planet, because we are jetting out of here. There won't be any floating up through the ceiling, saying, "good-bye, good-bye." In the twinkling of an eye, we'll be caught up into the sky.

"As it happened in the days of Noah," is the way it will be when we're caught up in the air with the Lord. So how was it in the days of Noah? Let's read on:

> They were eating, they were drinking, they were marrying, they were being given in marriage, until the day that Noah entered the ark, and the flood came and destroyed them all (v. 27).

They were carrying on business as usual. But what kind of business was it? Genesis 6:5 tells us they were doing only evil continually. We don't know what kind of evil was actually being done, so let's read on:

> It was the same as happened in the days of Lot: they were eating, they were drinking, they were buying, they were selling, they were planting, they were building; but on the day that Lot went out from Sodom it rained fire and brimstone from heaven and destroyed them all (vv. 28-29).

Where did Lot live? That's right, Sodom and Gomorrah. They, too, were carrying on business as usual. But what kind of business was it? In Jude 7 it tells us they were involved in gross immorality and were chasing after strange flesh.

Do you remember the story about the angels who went to rescue Lot? Oh, how that man loved the nightlife in Sodom. He didn't want to leave until morning. So the angels, who looked like men, decided to sleep in the city park. Lot nixed that idea. The angels weren't quite sure why Lot was so emphatic, but they agreed to sleep at Lot's house. They found out why in the middle of the night. The men of the town were homosexuals and came to Lot's house to rape his guests (see Gen. 19).

It was the last straw before God destroyed the city, all except for one family—Lot's.

It will be just the same on the day that the Son of Man is revealed (v. 30).

What was the last straw in the days of Lot before God destroyed everything except for one family? Sexual sin. What was the last straw in the days of Noah before God destroyed everything except for Noah's family? Sexual sin. And what will be the last straw in the final days just before our Lord comes back and destroys everything except for one family—His Church? Sexual sin! And how is it today? Sexually gross. We've got our Sodom in Las Vegas and our Gomorrah in San Francisco. It's almost time for God's "too-doo" to make its sound.

What's the point? In the Old Testament there is only one other thing for which God destroyed so utterly and completely—idol worship. But do you remember what he called it? Spiritual adultery (see Exod. 34:15). That's heavy stuff and a principle is wrapped up inside: Sexual sin is the negative standard by which the severity of all other sin is measured.

Like it or not immorality is a big deal with God. And woe to the person who doesn't get the message. Remember the concept of mastery? The stronger the slavery the stronger the discipline necessary to change the behavior. Therefore, the consequences for violating God's sexual mandates will be tougher than for any other sin you can commit. It's best to do what's right because it pleases God, but sometimes a little fear isn't bad.

Christian leaders are dropping like flies to adultery and sexual promiscuity. People of stature and status toward whom we look for leadership are failing to stay pure. The result is their ministries are taken from them. Sure, in Christ they are forgiven. Repentance restores their relationship with the Holy Spirit, but their impact on the Body of Christ is seldom the same again. There is very little room for leaders to stray sexually. God does not want the dominoes to fall.

You may be saying, "Jay, I want to hear about the love of God. Don't preach the fear of God to me." Listen carefully. I have spent much of my life on the road, and there's been an occasion or two when it's just been a solid dose of the fear of God that's kept my nose clean. I have even gotten to the point of being willing to disobey God, but I was afraid of the consequences. I knew the outcome would be too severe. A time of physical pleasure followed by a few seconds of zing can never be a substitute for destroying a family, ruining a ministry and causing the dominoes who look to you to stumble and fall. Besides, the resulting footholds can cause so many problems.

There is a reason God hates sexual sin more than any other sin. Sexual sin messes with the mechanism of creation, and that's where eternal souls are created.

A time of physical pleasure followed by a few seconds of zing can never be a substitute for destroying a family, ruining a ministry and causing others to stumble and fall.

AN INTERNAL VIOLATION

God considers every other sin external in nature except sexual sin, which is considered an internal violation of the dwelling place of the Holy Spirit. God considers immorality as different from all other sins—it's distinct and unique. He said so:

Run away from sexual sin! No other sin so clearly affects the body as this one does. For sexual immorality is a sin against your own body. Or don't you know that your body is the temple of the Holy Spirit, who lives in you and was given to you by God? You do not belong to yourself, for God bought you with a high price. So you must honor God with your body (1 Cor. 6:18-20, *NLT*).

Immorality is put in a different category. I'm not sure why, but let me give you a guess. How long will the souls of my two children last? Forever! Whether they end up in heaven or hell, their souls will last forever. My wife and I made something that is going to last forever. Not even the angelic host can do that or make that claim. Just us. And since making eternal souls is such an unusual privilege, as best as I can tell, God doesn't want the mechanism of creation violated until it is in the sanctity of the marriage bed, especially when the sins of the father are visited upon the children (see Exod. 34:7). God considers sex to be holy ground, and it's not to be violated. I guess that's why Satan is always so quick to make footholds out of our foul-ups.

If God hates sexual sin so much, and if He considers it to be so unique, there must be more to immorality than meets the eye. There is.

MORE THAN MEETS THE EYE

To understand what happens during immoral intercourse, it's necessary to understand the word "cleave." Cleaving is not putting two pieces of paper together and separating those two pieces of paper, or putting two boards together and separating those two boards. Instead, it's like the two components of Epoxy glue. Once you stir them together, they have cleaved and can't be separated into two parts again, at least not in the same way they existed before bringing them together.

Paul was referring to the word "cleave" when he used the phrase "the two shall become one flesh":

Don't you realize that your bodies are actually parts of Christ? Should a man take his body, which belongs to Christ, and join it to a prostitute? Never! And don't you know that if a man joins himself to a prostitute, he becomes one body with her? For the Scriptures say, "The two are united into one." But the person who is joined to the Lord becomes one spirit with him (1 Cor. 6:15-17, NLT).

Paul said that intercourse intertwines the participants. In a sense they become one body, and they will never be the same again once separated. That's good in the sanctity of the marriage bed since sexual intimacy between couples is facilitated in ways no other act can accomplish. But outside of God's blessing, the consequences are detrimental and can be lifelong.

The world says sex is just physical. Hopefully you enjoyed it, and when it's over that's it. But sex is more than physical bonding. You are body, soul and spirit (see 1 Thess. 5:23). Emotions are either a part of the soul or the spirit (probably the soul). That makes it impossible to cleave and not have an emotional intertwining. When the intertwining occurs out of wedlock, a scar is always produced. I call this scar a monster. In Amnon's case it was a monster of bitterness produced through intercourse.

YOU CAN STOP

Amnon, David's son, had a half sister named Tamar. Tamar was a "fox." We're talking the cutest—and she was a virgin. Virgins were rare commodities in those days too. Amnon wanted her desperately and sexually fantasized about her every day to the point of making himself sick. He got "ouchies" in his side. (That's a serious paraphrase of 2 Samuel 13:1-2.)

Let me put what happened to Amnon in modern-day terms. The parents of a high school girl go out for the evening, so she calls her boyfriend over to watch a little television. There are no éclairs in her refrigerator; she's not in a double-minded condition. She just wants to spend part of an evening with her boyfriend.

He shows up; they turn on the tube and watch *Cosby*. Halfway through the young couple enjoys a little kissy-face and huggy-bod, but that's it. It's no big deal—to her way of thinking anyhow. However, mastery has overcome him.

If you are a young man, I'm going to blow your cover in this particular situation. Our stallion repeats a standard line for guys at times like that. He says, "Don't stop me now, you can't stop me now, because if you stop me now, it's going to hurt me. So don't stop me now, you've got to keep going, because we've gone too far. We've got to go all the way, because if you stop me now, it will hurt me."

The young lady thinks about what he said, but as she ponders headlights from her folks' car flash through the living room window as they pull into the driveway, home unexpectedly early.

Here's a question for you: Could the guy stop or not? You bet he could! What was the situation when her folks walked into the house? Was everything cool? You bet your sweet begonias. Were there any problems? Are you kidding? Nobody suspected a thing.

Could the guy stop? Of course. Did he think he could stop? Nope, at least not until his reason for stopping was greater than his desire to press on. And when he got home that night the worst thing that might have happened would have been a little twinge in his side. He might have had to rest for a little while with one knee bent before falling asleep, but that's all that would have happened. Really! That's it.

Ladies, I hope you don't get yourselves into situations like that, but if a guy ever lays that line on you, just say, "Oh, no you don't. Go on home and take a cold shower. At the worst all you'll have is a little ouchie in your side, but it won't be any big deal. I'll see you later."

If you work at an office with a mover type, draw your boundaries early. Don't let familiarity change your standards. If you're in high school, decide what behaviors are pleasing to God and don't change them. If you're in a boring marriage, don't allow your situation to alter God's standards for you. Don't cave in. Compromise is a cruncher as you will see. That's why your rules have to be established at the beginning of a relationship and reemphasized in your mind at the beginning of each evening. There is a principle involved: In the heat of passion, there are no rules.

Sexual activity captivates. It consumes. In passion and panic all rules go out the window. But remember the polar bear alert principle: *When your imagination comes in conflict with your will, your imagination will usually prevail.* You most often end up doing a variation of that which you think about the most. That's what happened to Amnon.

TAMAR'S COMPROMISES

Amnon refuses to stop thinking about getting Tamar into bed, so he goes to his friend and asks him for advice. His buddy tells him, "Call your old man on the phone and tell him you're sick and that you need Tamar to come over and make some hot cakes for you so you will feel better."

Amnon thinks that's a great idea so he calls his dad and tells him he's got a bad case of the punies. When David arrives at his son's bachelor pad, Amnon fakes the flu and says something like, "Gee, Dad, I'm really sick. Would you send Tamar over here to care for me? I need some help. Some hot cakes would sure make me feel better, and nobody makes hot cakes better than Tamar" (see 2 Sam. 13:6).

Being a rather typical out-of-touch, out-to-lunch dad, David falls for it and sends for Tamar to make some hot cakes for Amnon. Do you think I'm kidding about the hot cakes? I'm not. Read verse six:

> So Amnon lay down and pretended to be ill; when the king came to see him, Amnon said to the king, "Please let my sister Tamar come and make me a couple of cakes in my sight, that I may eat from her hand."

See, hot cakes. You thought I was kidding. Not me. No sir!

So Tamar goes to her brother's house; he is lying down. She takes the Aunt Jemima pancake mix and makes that boy some flapjacks (see v. 8).

Then Amnon paints a pained look on his face, holds his arm to his brow and fakes agony as he says, "Tamar, I can't stand the noise from all the servants. All day long they've been making a clamor. Dismiss them for me will you? Send them away. I can't stand it anymore. Thanks so much" (see v. 9).

He sneaks a peek and then adds, "No, you stay please. I'll need some help with the cakes." Why does she stay? Have you ever thought about that? No? I think I know.

Tamar has no intention of going to bed with Amnon, although it is kind of fun to be there—in his condo. After all it is her dad who sends her there. I think the biggest reason she stays is that Amnon makes her feel desirable. She doesn't always feel that way. But feelings can get you into big trouble.

Most of us have self-image problems these days. That's why we are so susceptible to anyone who makes us feel attractive. Tamar feels "zing, zong, zing," and little goose bumps form on her arms—she likes feeling desirable—so she stays. She compromises just a little. Tamar doesn't realize that goose bumps and hot cakes don't mix.

Groaning, Amnon speaks again, "Oh, I think it's the Hong Kong flu. I'm so weak Tamar; I can't even move my hand to my mouth. Would you bring the food in here and feed me please? No joke, I'm wasted. I'm really sick." He takes another peek to see if she is falling for it. She is (see v. 10).

If he'd called her on the phone and said, "Tamar, would you come over here and go to bed with me?" she would have laughed in his face. But because of some feelings, she's in his bedroom, alone with him, and he's in bed. That's the situation after just two compromises.

Tamar doesn't intend what is about to happen to happen. He's the snake; he's the toad. I'm not blaming Tamar. He's premeditated this thing; he's the bad guy. But had Tamar fulfilled her obligation to her spiritual authority, she would have gotten out of there after she made the cakes. She could have, but the goose bumps got her. Now it's too late. Amnon grabs her and says, "Come, lie with me, my sister" (v. 11).

Tamar screams, "No, don't do this terrible thing!" and means it. There is no double-mindedness; she wants out of there. But he is stronger. He pulls her to himself and rapes her (see v. 14).

I don't want the women to hear me putting any blame on Tamar (so many women are abused along the way), but in this case she has the opportunity to leave. But because Tamar likes the way she feels, she stays a little longer than she should. Goose bumps can be expensive. *Compromise will get you into big trouble.* Amnon stages his plan and Tamar makes the necessary compromises. The cost of goose bumps can be high. Tamar finds that out—too late. It is too late for Amnon, too. Neither will be the same.

AMNON'S MONSTER

Sexual relationships outside of marriage rarely last, and people's attitudes change after having premarital sex. That's the way it is for Amnon after he rapes Tamar. He gets a scar—a monster of bitterness:

> Then Amnon hated her with a very great hatred; for the hatred with which he hated her was greater than the love [lust] with which he had loved [lusted after] her. And Amnon said to her, "Get up, go away! . . . throw this woman out of my presence, and lock the door behind her" (vv. 15,17).

The person who cares the least about the relationship has the most amount of power in it.

What's Amnon's attitude toward Tamar after he's had her? "Get up, go away, get out of my sight; you make me sick; I hate your guts," is essentially what he says. That's pretty strong talk. Amnon is not the same. His feelings have changed. And it happened after he had sex. Bitterness is the outcome of his sexual encounter.

The person who cares the least about the relationship has the most amount of power in it. A physical relationship alone will not keep ahold of a person. A man or a woman who tries to hang on to a member of the opposite sex with his or her body will end up being despised and usually cast aside.

Don't miss this message. It happens all the time. It's so easy to mistake lust for love. *Sure, I'll put out for him because he loves me,* the young high school girl thinks. But after he gets what he wants, the mystique is gone. He hates her for being easy and casts her aside. The next day at school she has to face him—knowing he knows her most intimate secrets and that his friends know also. She, too, becomes bitter.

The principle these high schoolers experienced applies to all ages, including folks who are currently married. Did you have sex with your spouse prior to the sanctity of marriage? Was physical attraction the basis of your relationship? If you answered yes to either question, have you ever wondered about the subtle hostility that exists between you as a couple? The reason is the principle found in 2 Samuel 13: Bitterness is the outcome of *premarital* sexual encounters.

If you got married on the basis of a physical relationship, the chances are that you got divorced. The thrill lasted probably 9 to 14 months. Figure six months of discouragement, a few months to decide, several months of processing the papers, and you found yourself divorced within two to three years. But if you happen to still be together, if the mandate not to divorce has prevailed in your life, you've had some tough times over the years, haven't you?

Why does bitterness exist between you? Where did it come from? Could it be a foothold of oppression from your immoral past? Probably! If so it's a monster of bitterness (see Appendix).

MIND MONSTERS

Monsters take form in ways other than bitterness. Those who have been promiscuous may have visual images of past encounters unexpectedly pop into their minds—and sometimes at the most inopportune times. It's like taking a trip through a grotesque art gallery, only you never know when you're going. That image is a monster, and the trip is a consequence of sin. Satan's agent is the tour guide.

Perhaps you've used pictures to stimulate yourself sexually. Do you occasionally have flashbacks? Older men actually have flashbacks to the pictures of their youth. Women flash to the romance they'd once hoped for. Why? You cannot look at a person with lust in your heart without committing adultery or fornication (see Matt. 5:28). Lusting after pictures creates an emotional intertwining—a visual monster, a scar. People hooked on pornography know the reality of mind monsters; scars are part of the consequences of sexual sin.

IT'S NEVER THE SAME AFTERWARD

Things are never the same after illicit sex of any kind. Scott found that out the hard way.

Four high school guys were out looking for a little fun—two seniors, a junior and Scott, who was a sophomore and the starting quarterback for the football team. The older three decided to get some beer. "The evening will be more fun with half a case to 'sip' on," they said.

Scott had never had a beer but he didn't want to look like a sissy in the eyes of his new friends, so he had a few. *It's no big deal,* he thought. Then the driver pulled a little bottle of pills out of his coat, took one and passed them on. He wanted to have more fun than beer could produce. Each of the guys took one, including Scott. Although he had never done uppers before, he wanted to be one of the guys. *One little compromise. What will it hurt? My folks will never find out,* he thought.

Then someone lit up and passed a joint. Scott took a hit. *What could happen? Is it really any worse than alcohol?* he asked himself.

Looking for something a bit more exciting, they decided to cruise lovers' lane. Seeing a lonely car with a two-headed body in the front seat, the three upperclassmen silently crawled up to the vehicle. Scott lagged behind a bit. The three jumped to their feet and yelled, trying to scare the occupants. Then they began bouncing the car. When the driver got out and approached one of them, the other two jumped him and hit him, and hit him and hit him, just for fun, until he lay helpless on the ground.

And then, just for fun, they put a bag over the girl's head and took turns raping her. First the two seniors, then the junior and then they called for Scott. It seemed like the thing to do. All the guys had done it. He did want to be accepted. Being high provided a good excuse.

But as he finished, the girl, who had been motionless and whimpering, began to flail and fight. As she did the bag came off her head and her eyes met Scott's eyes.

The girl he had just raped was his sister.

Compromise had taken its escalating toll and things would never be the same. Scott would be changed. Certainly his sister would be marred. The sister's boyfriend lost an eye from the beating; he would never be the same. I assume the three older guys now have prison records, and they must be very different too.

I don't know what happened to Scott or his sister. I never saw a follow-up article in the paper, but certainly their looks and glances at each other would be forever different.[1] Compromise caused it. Intercourse sealed it. God's most intimate act had been violated; relationships would forever be altered.

Scott's example is a violent one. So is Amnon and Tamar's. Even though Beth, Randy and Jack's example isn't violent, they'll all be different. And so will the girl who put out for the guy who said he loved her. The reason? When two unmarried people agree to have sex together, when it's over, it's not over. They will never be the same.

Like gravity it's one of God's rules.

Even though things will never be the same, there is a cure. There is a way to fix it. Not all of it of course. You understand that you cannot undo a pregnancy, reestablish virginity or get rid of AIDS. And deep emotional scars always leave a mark. But you can fix it—in God's eyes—and remove the footholds of the enemy. There is that kind of a cure, if you want it, which is the subject of the next chapter.

PULLING IT TOGETHER

1. Satan's goal is to pervert the things of God, especially the important things. Satan's primary goal is taking the virginity of our young people. His next objective is to involve as many as possible in immorality, because sexual purity is so important to God.

2. God hates sexual sin more than any other sin and considers it to be uniquely different. It's a violation of the dwelling

place of the Holy Spirit and of the sanctity of the mechanism of the creation of eternal things. As a result consequences for sexual sin are greater than for any other sin.

3. Sexual union is more than a physical happening. Emotions are involved. Intertwining occurs.

4. Compromise is the usual method of stumbling into sexual sin. Therefore, set your standards and keep them. Set them early and don't change them during the relationship. And remember, a physical relationship alone will not keep ahold of a person.

5. Bitterness is the outcome of premarital sexual encounters and is probably the reason so many men are harsh with their wives.

6. Mind monsters are memory scars that are part of the consequences of sexual sin.

7. After immoral sex things can never be the same.

Note

1. This story comes from a newspaper account from several years ago. I was unable to locate the original source.

CHANGING IMMORAL BEHAVIOR

CHAPTER EIGHT

Have you sinned sexually?

Do you now understand the magnitude of what happened and the resulting consequences?

I hope so. But take heart. I have very good news. God forgives sin, *but there is a catch.* There is a cure, but God puts a little hook in the deal. The woman at Jacob's well (see John 4:5-42) found out what I'm talking about. So did the prostitute at the Temple (see John 8:2-11). Here are my versions of their stories.

A LESSON FROM NANCY

Nancy was an office manager for a lawyer in southeast Los Angeles, on Central Avenue, not far from Rosecrans Boulevard, across from the city park. In her late 20s she loved to party. Nancy was a confident, liberated woman, who did what she wanted to do when she wanted to do it. She had lived with five different guys in as many years, but so what? Her churchgoing mother didn't approve, but that's the way it goes. Nancy was an adult and did as she pleased.

It had been rainy in L.A. for a couple of weeks. That was unusual. But today was a beauty, and Nancy looked out the window and noticed the park bench facing the bright warmth of the sun. *Today*, she resolved, *I'll enjoy my lunch on that bench. What a great day to eat outside.*

It was hard to concentrate on the briefs she was typing. Nancy knew she lacked purpose in life. She'd been thinking a lot about that lately and was surprised by the frequency. She had to stuff her thoughts more often to get her work done.

At 11:50 A.M. she noticed a group of motorcycle riders enter the parking lot. They weren't Hell's Angels types. These guys were hog riders atop big, full dress, road bikes. The leader went to Nancy's bench while the others went off in several directions.

Nobody's gonna spoil my plans, Nancy confidently thought to herself.

At noon she went to Mickey D's and got a Big Mac, fries and a Coke. When she got back to the park the guy was still there, at one end of the bench. Nancy went to the other end and sat. After all it was the only bench facing the sun.

She reached into the sack and pulled out the Coke. Then she grasped the straw. Thoughts of shooting the guy with the straw wrapper entered her mind and she smirked at the thought. She didn't of course. The first gulp was marvelous; the blast of carbonation is always terrific. Her throat burned wonderfully for a few moments.

Next came the Big Mac. Nancy lifted the lid and dumped the fries into the empty half of the burger container, because that's where you put them when you've ordered a Big Mac, fries and a Coke. She then removed a package of ketchup from the sack. Nancy thought about dropping the packet on the ground and stomping on it, which would shoot ketchup all over him. How fun! She didn't of course, but her smirk gave her away again. She liked the thought.

When she picked up her burger, it happened. The guy asked, "Nancy, can I have a drink of your Coke?"

Who is this guy? she thought. *He doesn't live around here. I don't know him and I don't want to know him; I don't want anything to do with him. But how in the world does he know my name?* she wondered.

Her first thoughts were of the liquid going up the straw—and then back down the straw having touched him. Yuck! What if he took the lid off and put his mouth on the side? Fluid would touch his lips and go back into the cup—backwash for sure. It's one thing to share a Coke with a boyfriend, but it's quite another to share one with a stranger.

"How dare you be forward with me? I don't know you and I don't want to know you."

"Nancy, God loves you."

"How do you know my name?"

"You've been thinking a lot about the three big questions of life lately: Where did I come from; Why am I here; and Where am I going? Isn't that true?"

"Yeah, but how'd you know?"

"Why don't you get your husband so I can tell you about myself and the life I have to offer."

"I'm not married," she said, calming down at the sound of his voice.

"You said that right. You've had five men in your life in the last five years."

"What are you—some kinda know it all?"

Nancy's head was spinning. This guy was causing a serious systems error in the computer between her ears. He knew about her life, and the look in his eyes confirmed his awareness of the guilt she felt from violating her upbringing. Her momma had taught her how to live right, but she wasn't. He knew it, and she knew it, too.

There was no denying the unusual nature of the man. No, that wasn't quite right. He was more than unusual. "Do you know about God?" she asked without thinking.

"I who speak to you am He."

The look in his eyes as he said those words made bells, gongs, buzzers and whoops go off in her head. Bingo! It was like looking at the snake on the stick in Numbers 21. Those who looked were saved from juences of snakebite. Nancy had looked at Christ, and when coupled with her repentant heart, the combination became energizing, saving faith. She was cured from the snakebite of sin.

The other bikers showed up with Chicken McNuggets for the boss. They were a little concerned about him being alone and talking to a woman in this neighborhood, because they assumed her to be a prostitute.

Nancy was so excited that she dashed off to the office to get her friends. She had just met Jesus and wanted what had just happened to her to happen to them. Although she had lived with five different men in the past five years, Nancy felt clean and forgiven—and in fact was.

Did Jesus die for all sin except sexual? Nope. Jesus died for all sin—period.

Then does Jesus forgive adultery and fornication? You bet!

Have you committed sexual sin in your past? Perhaps you're in the middle of an immoral relationship right now.

I have very good news. Jesus died for all sin, including immorality. Believe it and repent. Forgiveness is yours if you want it. Here's the catch: You will have to want a relationship with Jesus more than you want to continue in sin—you will have to believe as well as repent.

That's what Nancy did. The woman at the Temple did, too.

A TERRIFIC TIME AT THE TEMPLE

In John 8, Jesus was teaching at the Temple when the religious leaders brought forth a woman who had been caught in adultery.

"Teacher," they used the word irreverently. "This woman has been caught in adultery, in the very act. Now in the Law, Moses commanded us to stone such women; what then do You say?" (vv. 4-5). (Stoning, in this sense, means throwing rocks at a person until they die.)

Jesus bent over and began to doodle in the sand. They kept after Him for an answer, so He stood and said, "Let those of you who have never been immoral throw the first rock" (see v. 7). Then He bent over and doodled again.

You're in for a treat. I know what Jesus doodled. That's right. Are you ready for this revelation? Here goes.

The first time Jesus doodled in the sand, He drew valentine hearts. That's right. You read correctly, and you read it here first. Valentine hearts. The second time He doodled, He filled in the hearts.

The oldest guy there was named George—George the Jew. Jesus wrote in the first heart: "George + Gertrude."

George was shocked. Nobody knew about Gertrude. It had been years and years ago. Everyone who knew about it was dead by now, even Gertrude. How did this guy know? George didn't know how He knew, but the fact that He did know made it impossible for him to throw the first stone. Old George left.

The second oldest guy there was named Ronald—Ronald the Rabbi. Jesus wrote in the second heart: "Ronald + Mary Belle." Ronald thought to himself, *How does He know about Mary Belle? That was just last week at the Rabbi's convention, and He wasn't even there.* There was no way he would start the game by throwing the first rock with this guy aware of his hypocrisy. He split too.

And on it went—heart after heart, from the oldest to the youngest, until they all had left. Jesus asked, "Woman, where are they? Did no one condemn you?" (v. 10).

"No one, Lord." (She used a word meaning "Savior.") Jesus replied, "I do not condemn you, either. Go. From now on sin no more" (v. 11).

"Go on about your business but stop sleeping around" was the essence of Jesus' words.

Believing her Lord was one of the two keys to her receiving forgiveness. Her desire to please Jesus by ceasing her sin was the other. The woman believed, repented and received salvation.

GOOD NEWS

If you have been involved in immorality, I have very good news for you: In Jesus Christ your sin is *forgiven*.

What did Jesus tell the woman as she left the Temple? Go, and stop committing sexual sin. In other words, change your heart, quit going that way, stop, turn and face me. Run toward me. If you can't run, walk. If you stumble or slide back three or four steps for every step forward, just keep crawling. If you face me, you're okay. Your heart controls the direction you're facing; it's your heart I care about.

Repentance is a change of heart. Without it you'll end up with éclairs in your refrigerator. And if you haven't decided to stop committing sexual sin, there isn't much that can be done about your footholds either.

Repentance is a change of heart. Without it you'll end up with éclairs in your refrigerator.

BREAKING BAD HABITS

Would you like to give your body to Christ and to moral purity regardless of your past?

Are you afraid to go for the total forgiveness God has for you because of habit patterns established in your life?

Are you afraid you might fall back into sin next week or next month, so you don't want to do anything now?

Maybe you've been to a church summer camp and rededicated your life. Then you descended the mountain and messed up. So at winter camp you rededicated your life again. Then you descended the mountain and messed up again. And so it goes, year after year, and you don't want to play that game with God anymore, or yourself for that matter, ever again. I understand.

Here is a solution to your habit problem. *Figure out where you lose control and then back up one step*. If it's hard for you to drive by that adult bookstore, then go home via another route. If soaps send you into sexual fantasy, don't turn on the TV, unplug it, watch CNN or ESPN, or put your foot through the screen. If the pictures on the magazines at 7-11 cause you some mental image problems, go to a different store. If the skin flick channel in the motel room is hard for you to keep from watching, check into a room that doesn't have a system in it. As a dating couple, if everything is cool until you park the car, then don't park the car. If that person turns you on, then don't go out with that person unless the behavior lines are carefully drawn.

I know. You've tried to quit before. This time can be different. This time will be different. You can break the cycle. This time you can break the habit pattern that leads you into sin. Backing up one step before mastery takes over will do it.

SEVENTY TIMES SEVEN

How many times will Jesus forgive you for committing the same sin over and over? It's an important question. What did He tell Peter?

Peter had put his foot in his mouth, as usual. He was trying to sound intelligent. That was Peter's first mistake. He also was being a bit prideful. That was the second.

Peter asked Jesus, "How many times should a person forgive?" He tried answering the question himself to be a big shot, "Seven" (see Matt. 18:21). Peter thought he was being generous. After all the law only required three.

Jesus popped his bubble when He said, "Seventy times seven" (v. 22). In other words, forgive as often as repentance is present. Forgive beyond all reasonable expectation. There's a principle in those words: God will generate forgiveness on our behalf for the same sin, over and over, as long as we come to Him in repentance.

You may think that if the behavior continues the person must not be repentant. But that's not necessarily so. People who overeat are usually genuinely sorry after they have eaten too much. They are trapped in a habit pattern. The habit doesn't excuse the sin, but it may make it difficult to alter their behavior without some time and help. The young man who masturbates and feels the resulting pangs of guilt or shame will vow to never do it again, and he means it. He is both sorry and repentant. But until he alters his activity pattern, the behavior will be very hard to break, because it is a habit. And if he has sexual fantasy, if mastery is demonstrated and if he does masturbate again, how many times will God forgive him if he addresses his heavenly Father in his weakness with a repentant heart? Seventy times seven; as many times as necessary.

DECREASING YOUR CONFESSION TIME

Asking for forgiveness while intending to go back and sin is not repentance. The Mafia hit man who goes to confession to acknowledge his last job but already has a new contract in his pocket has not demonstrated repentance. He has éclairs in his refrigerator. His heart hasn't changed. However, if your past has resulted in a habit pattern and in your heart of hearts you want to be pleasing to God, that is repentance, even though it may take several attempts to break the pattern.

I don't want you to say, "I'm never going to do that again." It would be great if you can do that. But if what you don't want to do is already a habit, it may be very difficult to change that habit. You may foul up a few times before you get the upper hand. Just don't give up because you mess up. You can win over an old habit; you really can. Just don't let a stumble be a defeat for you. Rather, turn it into a victory. Here's how: *Lengthen your time between stumbles and decrease the amount of time it takes you to confess.* The idea will turn potential defeats into victories.

Let's review what I told you in chapter 3 about the fight Mary and I had. When Mary and I fought our usual MO was to ignore each other for a few days. We had been working on improving that part of our relationship for a couple of months. However, a flare-up occurred. As we were going to bed, instead of retreating into my shell, I told her I was sorry for the way I handled the situation. She chuckled, smiled and said, "It's been a long time since that was a problem. Let's use this one as a measuring stick in order to lengthen the time to the next one." In other words, what would have been a defeat that would have normally sent us both spiraling down into several days of depression became a point of victory.

Purpose not to repeat your habit, but if you do mess up, measure the time between this one and the last. If the time between stumbles increases, you're winning.

Also, when you do foul up, how long does it take you to confess it? If the confession time decreases, you're winning.

Don't let one stumble send you on a downward spiral of defeat. One mess up does not indicate defeat. Break habits by lengthening the time between stumbles and decreasing the time between confessions.

The issue is your heart, isn't it? None of the other issues matter. How is your heart? Is it hard toward God? He can't do much for you if it is. But if your heart is soft toward Him, if you have a heart yearning for Christ, accept His forgiveness for your past and work with Him on your future.

PULLING IT TOGETHER

1. In spite of the magnitude of your sexual offenses, God is eagerly waiting to forgive you, and He will if you just change your heart and demonstrate it by going about the business of changing your behavior.

2. If you are in the vise of a bad habit, the key is to alter your behavior before the point of lost control. Think through your behavior patterns and determine where you lose control. Then back up one step. Success should be measured by lengthening your time between stumbles. And if you do fall, you can progressively shorten the time before you confess. Both are evidence of a repentant heart.

GOD'S SOLUTION TO SEXUAL TEMPTATION

I was in the San Francisco Bay area and had just come back from speaking. I parked my car in the motel parking lot and saw a woman struggling with her luggage. It would have been unkind not to help her. She invited me into her room.

I didn't have a decision to make. I had already decided to set the bags down outside her door and go straight back to my room. I made that decision in the parking lot. But even so I required a little mental discipline. I still remember her room number—203. Flattery is an enticing commodity. Remember Tamar and the cost of goose bumps?

Since most people have messed up in sexual areas, let's look at the biblical solution to staying pure. There's only one: Ruuuunnnnn! Your passport to purity is a simple formula:

Purity = beat feet.

The solution to the temptation of sexual sin is a two-word mandate. First Corinthians 6:18 says, "Flee immorality." That's the best way to thump the devil's rump. Get out of there and don't sin in the first place.

Flee! Stay out of situations where trouble might find you. There is no other instruction. Just as God made only one way to Himself (through Jesus), and Christ reemphasized the point by saying spiritual birth must occur (you must be born again), God made only one way to handle sexual temptation. Run! Set your rules, etch them in stone and make sure you follow them, and then when temptation comes—scram.

You may think that I missed a great opportunity to share Jesus with a woman who probably didn't know Him. Not so. I had to run to be safe. Let God raise up a woman to share with her. He can send someone to get her into a church. At times like that His highest commandment for me is to bug out.

WE CAN'T BE TRUSTED

People need to learn to run from sexual sin, including *all situations that can lead to temptation.* It's the only solution God gives. He tells us to run because we can't be trusted.

I'm into Superman. I was raised on Superman. I think he's great. But in *Superman II,* Superman went to bed with Lois Lane. I was devastated. I couldn't believe he'd do a thing like that. Superman, my hero, the man of steel, rusted in front of my very eyes.

Folks, if you can't trust Superman, who can you trust? Do you know what I mean? And that's the point. When it comes to sexual temptation, nobody can be trusted. That's why there's only one instruction given as to how to handle sexual sin. Leave! Scram! Split! Jet! Get out of there! Never try to stand firm and be the mighty man or woman of steel. Because ultimately you will rust.

Ladies, remember when you were in high school and you had one of those talks with your folks when you wanted to stay out later than usual? They said no, but you were determined to go the limit to get your way. As the conversation progressed tears began falling down your cheeks, which led to sobbing, which led to mild convulsing sounds followed by deep whimpers. Remember? Finally, when you had run out of options, you resorted to the last weapon in your arsenal as you blurted out, "You (sniff), you (whimper, whimper), you just don't trust me (boo, hoo, hoo)!" Have you ever used that line on your folks? Just about every girl who has grown into womanhood has tried that one on her parents at one time or another.

Guys do it differently. They stand, looking Dad in the eye in a macho head-cocked-to-the-side stance, and say, "Hey, Dad, why don't you trust me? Huh? Huh?" They then tilt their chin upward in a snapping, defiant kind of motion three or four times for emphasis.

Let me tell you something that's very important. When it comes to sex, I want my kids to know something absolutely, for certain, for sure: I don't trust 'em! *I don't trust them because they can't be trusted.* And neither can you.

I was talking to an 85-year-old man the other day. I asked him, "When did you stop noticing the ladies?"

He said, "I haven't yet. Perhaps you need to talk to someone who's a little older."

We can't be trusted. That means there should always be a few precautions taken to protect relationships from sexual compromise.

POLICE YOURSELF

The best precaution I know of is to police yourself.

Kim was 17 and dating a fellow. (I asked my daughter's permission to tell this story.) I was impressed with him. He was a relatively new Christian and had given his testimony in church a few weeks before he called and asked for permission to date my daughter. That will dazzle any dad. When they went out I could see them pray in the car before they drove off. Sometimes they'd pray at the end of the evening before or after a little face pressing.

One day I asked my daughter, "Kim, how are you doing in your relationship with your boyfriend? Are you guys staying pure?" You have to have a pretty good relationship to ask your kid a question like that. God has given us that kind of a relationship.

"Yes, Dooley, (that's our word of special tenderness) we are," she replied. "A little kissy-face, a little huggy-bod, that's it. But we almost had a problem. When our dates ended early, say around 11, since I didn't have to be in until midnight (nobody wants to be in early), we would go park the car, talk and watch the 'submarine races.' There were no éclairs in our refrigerator. All we wanted to do was talk. But the longer we were together, the more things progressed and our emotions began to take over. The longer we were in the car, the closer we got and the more intimate we started to become. That's when we remembered what you said."

"Say what!" I exclaimed. I had never heard of a kid remembering anything her parents ever said, especially in a parked car. The sound of my mouth hitting the floor filled the room.

Kim continued, "You said we needed to believe we couldn't be trusted in the area of sex, and we believed you. So we went to a coffee shop and had a Pepsi. And that's what we do now. It's safer, 'cause we know we really can't be trusted."

Knock me over with a feather! A kid believed her dad. That's unheard of you know! She actually believed me. I may have gotten a snow job, but I don't think so, so I extended their closing hours.

There were no éclairs in Kim's refrigerator. All they really wanted to do was talk. And they wanted to protect themselves from what could have happened if they had responded to their feelings. So they went to a coffee shop, sat in a booth and had a soda. They policed themselves; it was a cinch because they weren't going to "get it on" in the booth. Policing yourself is another great way to thump the devil's rump because, just like running, you don't sin.

There are several other policing tactics that I'd like to suggest. Granted, some of these may be in variable areas and may be just fine for you, but look out. About the time you think you're safe is the time you're closest to falling.

Counseling

I tell pastors not to talk to another man's wife more than once in a counseling situation unless another woman is present or unless her husband is there. Why? Because neither the counselor nor the counseled can be trusted! Probably the biggest contributor to pastoral infidelity is the result of intimate, repeated, private counseling with women. Don't allow your pastor to do it. Make sure he's policing himself. Don't you do it either.

Praying

Never pray repeatedly with a member of the opposite sex unless you want the relationship to deepen. When I worked with large college departments in our previous churches, I found that when prayer partners were opposite sexes, their relationships usually went from friends to dating. *Married people should never pray repeatedly with a member of the opposite sex other than their spouses.* It's just too intimate—therefore, too dangerous. Police yourselves.

Hugging

I preach in quite a few churches where the people hug a lot. Some churches do some serious hugging. It's like greeting someone with a modern-day version of the biblical "holy kiss" Paul talked about, only they greet each other with a holy hug. It's the cultural thing to do and, in that environment, you can't avoid participating without being rude.

When I preach I represent God to the people and the people to God. Sometimes a woman sitting out there in the audience thinks, *Oh, what a godly man.* She doesn't know me. (The godliest person you know lives at least 150 miles away. Godly people are the ones you don't know very well, because after you get to know them, you usually find they aren't so godly.)

Sometimes a lady who thinks that way, who is part of a huggin' church, will get out of her seat and come straight at me after I finish speaking. She's thinking, *Oh, what a godly man.* I'm thinking, *Oh, what a woman*. Sometimes women forget that God wired men differently—and sometimes they know very well what they're doing.

At any rate here she comes. It's going to be a full-on, three-point body press for sure. My practice is to rotate 45 degrees to the side, put my left hand in my pocket and say, "Give me half a hug."

My actions say, "I care about you and I want to honor you, but let's make sure there is some godly distance between us. I want you to know I can't be trusted. I also want you to know that I don't trust you either." It's an effective policing action.

Call me old-fashioned but I never want my wife fully in somebody else's arms. I don't trust myself enough to allow somebody else's wife in mine. Many a spouse has a sinking heart when his or her mate fully embraces someone else.

Back Rubs

On college retreats or other singles' gatherings, lots of back rubs are given. Rubbing backs is socially acceptable petting, and it really is okay. Most handle it just fine, but it is a problem for some. Minds start racing. Fantasy is fueled. If it's a problem for you, don't participate. Police yourself.

In married circles back rubs may become more than therapy, and it is a practice that ought to be scrutinized carefully. I for one don't want another man's hands on my wife's body, and I'll keep my hands off theirs. It's a policing tactic.

What practices are you engaged in that fuel your fantasies and stimulate your senses? They may be legitimate activities and socially acceptable practices, but are they okay for you? Think through what policing action you need to take. You'll be staying on the offensive if you do.

ARE YOU PLAYING WITH FIRE?

If you are single the following questions probably don't apply to you. Your yes is most likely a healthy response. But for a married person, an affirmative answer could mean big trouble.

Is there a person at church you want to see on Sunday because you fantasize about him or her during the week?

Is there a person you look forward to hugging ahead of time? Is there a person you like to be around because he or she stirs your emotions?

Do you find yourself hanging around to watch somebody walk by?

Do you find yourself looking forward to a committee meeting because that person will be there?

Is there something about your counseling appointment that makes you especially look forward to it?

Are you a chronic back rubber or rubbee? Why?

Are you involved in any contact activity that might not be good for you?

If you answer yes to any of these questions, figure out how to run. You're playing with fire if you don't. A decision to keep messin' around is a decision that will probably lead to your downfall. And you're probably allowing Satan to gain a foothold in your life.

We've talked about the need to Ruuuunnnnn! and to police ourselves as methods to avoid immorality. But they are not enough if we've allowed footholds to be entrenched. It's now time to enter into war, to engage in battle. We'll do that in the next chapter.

PULLING IT TOGETHER

1. God offers only one solution to the problem of sexual temptation—don't allow yourself to be tempted. Run, avoid, stay
   away, leave, flee, turn it off, don't buy it and get out of there.
   Beat feet when sexual temptation comes. Running is God's
   only solution to dealing with sexual temptation.

2. Nobody can be trusted with sexual temptation. Pastors,
   counselors, neighbors, friends and relatives shouldn't be
   trusted. Too much time in the wrong setting will cause anyone to fall to sexual sin.

3. Since you know you can't be trusted, police yourself. Think
   through an evaluation of your high-risk areas and determine
   what you are going to do about them.

IT'S TIME TO THUMP THE DEVIL'S RUMP—PART 2

In David's day the local bookie, Jimmy the Philistine, took a lot of bets on Goliath. There was no action on David, not even from David's own army. But just as David and God made a "majority with authority," you and God can kick the devil, too, if you let the Father do the kickin' in the power of the Son. Stay behind your shield of faith as God goes to work on your behalf. You *will* come out a winner.

Since sexual immorality is the devil's area of emphasis, he most likely has brought up reinforcements in an attempt to hang on as long as he can. The battle usually takes a little longer when dealing with sins of immorality, so be patient. To counter Satan's defense, in addition to warfare, an "armoring-up" prayer has been added. Before beginning, if you need a faith boost, reread the biblical verses stating God's authority over the enemy from chapter 5.

Don't skip this procedure. Just because you dealt with anger doesn't mean you don't have to deal with immorality. The issues are different.

That's why there's a new set of instructions. As before pray and resist out loud with authority. It's time to counterattack.

ARMOR UP

The Bible talks about the armor that is ours to wear when we go into battle. All we have to do is put it on:

Finally, be strong in the Lord and in the strength of His might. Put on the full armor of God, so that you will be able to stand firm against the schemes of the devil. For our struggle is not against flesh and blood, but against the rulers, against the powers, against the world forces of this darkness, against the spiritual forces of wickedness in the heavenly places.

Therefore, take up the full armor of God, so that you will be able to resist in the evil day, and having done everything, to stand firm. Stand firm therefore, having girded your loins with truth, and having put on the breastplate of righteousness, and having shod your feet with the preparation of the gospel of peace; in addition to all, taking up the shield of faith with which you will be able to extinguish all the flaming arrows of the evil one. And take the helmet of salvation, and the sword of the Spirit, which is the word of God (Eph. 6:10-17).

We'll go into war with the enemy after we put on our armor. Pray the following prayer to armor up.

PRAYER

Heavenly Father, my desire is for You to come against my enemy, the devil. I am prepared, but I do not come in my own strength, but rather in the power of the risen Lord Jesus Christ. I come dressed in the whole

armor of God so that I may resist the devil and stand firm.
Therefore, I shield my vital areas with Your truth. Father,
I want righteousness to be the most obvious thing about me.
I will use it as a breastplate. Your gospel of peace shall be my shoes.
Thank You for faith to use as a shield to ward off Satan's assaults.
Finally, Lord, I take the helmet of salvation to cover my head, and I
take Your Word as my sword. So armed I am ready for battle.

BREAKING THE ENEMY'S GRIP

You are ready to continue. Initially you will be praying and resisting as
you did when you dealt with anger. As you get into it, the procedure will
then specifically deal with various kinds of immorality. You'll finish by
removing footholds. Continue out loud and with authority.

PRAYER

Father, I approach You in the name of Your Son, Jesus Christ, whose
name is above every name, and I call upon You. I acknowledge Your
sovereign authority and power over all creation, visible and invisible.
I rest fully in the assurance of Your love for me; I claim and stand on the
certainty that I belong to You, redeemed by the blood of Jesus Christ to
cleanse my sin and set me free from the accusations of Satan. I ask You,
Lord, in the authority of Jesus' name, to remove all enemy hindrance and
to clear a pathway for my prayer. Father, send angels to war against all
powers of darkness assigned to me. Tear down and destroy all schemes
and strongholds set up against my mind, will and emotions. Remove the
footholds of opportunity that were erected as the result of my sinful past.
Lord God, Your power has been fully invested in Jesus Christ,
and I ask that You bring that power against my enemy, the one
who hates You and therefore hates me, who is made in Your image.
Bring the power of the Resurrection, all the power of the

Glorification, all the power of the Ascension and all the power that raised up Christ to sit at Your right hand against my foe.

RESIST

In Christ, I stand firm against all enemies of Jesus Christ sent against me, and I ask the Father to bring them into the light of judgment of the holy One of Israel. Expose their schemes, place them under the sovereign power and judgment of the Lord Jesus Christ, and shatter their influence. Father, command Satan and all enemies of Jesus Christ under his charge to prepare to leave me alone. Bring the power of the blood of Jesus Christ against them. Defeat them in the name of the eternal God, the Father of all glory, the Son Jesus Christ, and the Spirit of truth and perfect light.

You are now ready to break footholds and take back old ground.

You may begin to demonstrate some physical or emotional symptoms at this point. Classically, gooseflesh may come over you in waves, accompanied by fear. Keep in mind that fear is not from the Father, and it is evidence of the power of God disrupting the enemy's foothold. You can come against the fear, as it cannot stand in front of the power invested in Jesus Christ. You may also feel dizzy or light-headed, have an increased heartbeat, feel tightness in the chest, or even have some difficulty breathing or talking. Don't stop; those are probably signs of angelic activity in the supernatural realms warring on your behalf in the name and power of Jesus Christ.

PRAYER

Pray about each of the following issues.

Is sexual fantasy a problem for you? Do you think about sexual things during your free time, as you're drifting off to sleep, as you wake up early in the morning or when you're riding in the car? Ask God about those questions right now. Will you ask the Spirit of God to stimulate your mind so that you might have a polar bear alert of sorts when fantasy comes, and will you purpose to lengthen your time between stumbles and decrease your time between confessions? Will you determine with the help of the Holy Spirit to decrease this habit little by little until it is under control? Will you acknowledge your need for God's help and also realize the importance of exercising your will to gain control of sexual fantasy in your life? Has God convicted you about the need to take your thoughts captive in this area? Will you respond by saying yes? Or are you praying in a double-minded condition with éclairs in your refrigerator, not really wanting or intending to respond to God's prompting? *Pray on your own about sexual fantasy and what God wants you to do about it before continuing.*

Is pornography a problem? Do sexy movies, skin videos, sensual television shows, hot magazines and provocative novels cause you difficulty? What are you going to do about them? Will you destroy the literature right now? What about the videos and DVDs? Will you burn them so that no one else will be affected? Will you purpose not to watch those shows? Will you disconnect the cable if you don't have control? *Pause and ask God what He wants you to do in the area of pornography before continuing.*

Are you a flirt? I don't mean the casual flirtation between two teenagers getting to know each other. Rather, do you dress, carry yourself, speak to, and bump or rub against people in ways that are intended to turn them on? Is that you? You should stop. *Will you confess your flirtation and give it up?*

Are you currently involved in a petting relationship with someone to whom you are not married? Your times together are getting "handsier and handsier," aren't they? I know you like it, especially when your back goes zing, zong, zing. And I know you like the feel of goose bumps. But do you realize where it's leading, that you can't be trusted and if you aren't already, you're close to dishonoring the Lord? Will you stop? And if you can't stop, will you give your partner up if necessary because it's the right thing to do before God? Do you love the Lord and His commandments more than you love that person? *Make your choice now before continuing.*

Are you currently involved in a sexual relationship with someone with whom you are not married? Are you caught up in how good it feels and at the same time struggling with the guilt of it all? Regardless of your circumstances will you determine to give that person up because it's right before God? Will you repent? *Pray about that before continuing.*

You now need to ask God, once and for all, to forgive you for your past sexual sins, including the loss of your virginity (if you lost it). *Confess each sin as the Holy Spirit brings it to mind. Pray on your own. (This may take some time, so linger awhile in prayer and wait on the Lord.) Confess now.* When you have finished confessing, continue praying:

> *God, I give myself to You and to the moral purity You desire. Today, (fill in the date), is my date of forgiveness.*

And when Satan hits you with a memory from your past, ask God to help you to remember to rebuke him by commanding:

> No, Satan, I asked forgiveness for that, and I know what you are trying to do. Lord Jesus, I'm under attack. Come and take authority over my enemies. Make them leave in Jesus' name!

Enter today's date in your Bible.

Remember this about what you just did. How many times do you have to ask forgiveness for a sin if you confess it with a repentant heart? That's right, only once! So in the future when a voice comes along and reminds you of a sin you have previously confessed, whose voice is it? It's not God's. Have a polar bear alert to take the thought captive, pray and then resist.

PART 3:

WARFARE TO BREAK FOOTHOLDS OF GODLESSNESS— ARE YOU CHASING AFTER WIND?

Jacob was a mamma's boy, a homebody and fancied himself to be a gourmet cook. He was into natural foods and veggies. His specialty was red lentil stew. Jacob also was a liar and a sneak.

Esau was a man's man. He drove a big-wheeled pickup with mags, hung a rifle in his rear window, wore a baseball cap and loved to hunt. But he thought religion was a crutch and cared little about the things of God.

The Lord had promised Jacob the birthright, but Esau had been born first, so it was legally his. Jacob knew God would work it out eventually, but he figured the Lord might need his help; besides, things were moving too slowly to suit this ambitious schemer.

Esau came home from hunting one day. He had forgotten to take his lunch and was famished. Absolutely starved to the bone, he was. Thought he was going to die, he did. Walking through the door he sniffed the air and, to his delight, smelled his favorite delicacy—red lentil stew. Esau loved it, and nobody but nobody made this cooking-pot delight better than Jacob. However, Esau kept his love for natural foods very private in order to preserve his macho image among his friends. Nobody knew it, but Esau actually liked quiche.

Esau bellowed from the back porch, "Jacob, I'm home and I'm starved," as the screen door slammed. "Is that what I think it is? I like what my nose smells. That's red lentil stew. Can I have some? I got skunked hunting today and missed lunch to boot. I can't ever remember being this hungry. What do you say?"

Jacob had already thought this conversation through. He knew what he would say and how he was going to say it. "Sure," he said matter-of-factly, "if you'll give me the birthright." He continued on, "You don't really care about it anyhow. Tell you what. You give me the birthright and I'll give you the whole pot of stew."

To say that Esau was shortsighted would be a gross understatement, because in essence Esau demonstrated his disregard for the things of God by trading his birthright for a full stomach. He swapped salvation for stew. He took gas over God. As a result of his pursuit, Esau got a foothold (see Gen. 25:27-34).

So many times the immediacy of the moment seems to dominate our values. We settle for too little and for things that are so temporal. Two Old Testament phrases address that issue. The first is "vanity of vanities" (Eccles. 1:2). In my own words it means "bubbles." Something appears to be there, but with a "Pop!" it's gone. There's not much left after a bubble bursts. It's like breath on a window; it disappears as we watch. The second is "chasing after the wind" (Eccles. 1:14, *NIV*). Think of taking a cardboard box outside and scooping up the breeze. Then bring the box inside, pull back the flaps and wait for your hair to blow back. It's a long wait isn't it?

Bubbles and wind are the things in life that replace Christ as the most important. Do you have any bubbles in your life? Are you spending too much time chasing after the wind? Life is a series of choices. Heaven or hell is the result of a choice. So is the power of the Holy Spirit. Although most of you have worked through the biggies, choosing between better and best gets real tough sometimes. However, the choices you make demonstrate your priorities.

YOUR "CONE" MAY HAVE THE WRONG PRIORITIES

Your life is like a cone. At the base there's plenty of room for almost everything, but as you come up the side from the base, the circumference diminishes, forcing you to make some choices. Only the important things in your life remain as you approach the top. The big question is: What's on the top of the cone of your life? If it isn't Jesus then whatever is there is keeping you from coming to Christ if you don't know Him. If you're a believer it is grieving and quenching God's Holy Spirit in you. And whatever it is represents godlessness (anything more important to you than Christ).

Figuring out what's on top is like having a fire in your home and only having enough time to take one armload of stuff out with you before everything else burns. What would you take? Things or memories? The computer or your pictures? Maybe it depends on your age. If your kids were in the house, getting them out would be crucial, wouldn't it? Whatever you took would be the most important thing to you. It's that way with life too.

Whatever you think about the most must be the most important thing to you. For many, striving after money, goals, desires and dreams is like chasing after the wind. And all they get are footholds for their efforts.

MONEY CAN BE WIND

A rich young ruler approached Jesus one day. "What must I do to be saved?" he asked. You can see he knew something was wrong. Even though he had everything the world had to offer, he knew it wasn't enough. Something was missing. His innards confirmed the danger, so he went to ask Jesus about what was absent in his life.

Jesus strung him along and avoided the main issue in order to deepen their relationship and develop rapport between them. He avoided the young man's question with a question. "How are you doing with the law?" He asked.

"Great!" The young man was excited because he was a good guy and knew it; therefore, if being good was the criteria for eternal life, he was all set.

But Jesus threw him a curveball when He said, "That's wonderful. Now get rid of all your money and follow Me."

By the way there was only one other man, Thomas, Jesus ever looked at like He looked at this man. The look is described as a long, loving, drawing, compelling, pulling kind of look, filled with deep love, concern and compassion. Thomas responded to Jesus' expression with the words, "My Lord and my God!" (John 20:28), a far different response than was given by the young, yuppie politician, who said, "Oh my God!" It wasn't a prayer. For this Jewish entrepreneur it was a statement of exclamation. *Such a price,* he thought. *It's just too high.* Then the rich kid turned and sadly walked away (see Matt. 19:16-22). His bucks were at the top of his cone and a foothold was in his life. He could have traded his dollars in for eternal life. But he made a bad deal like Esau, who took gas over God. Money can be so expensive and, like wind, it's just not worth chasing.

BUCKS AREN'T BAD UNLESS THEY'RE AT THE TOP

Did you ever notice that Jesus never asked Joseph of Arimathea or Nicodemus to give up their money? Why? Because money wasn't the issue; it's still not the issue. Whatever is more important to a person than Jesus Christ is the issue. Therefore, in Joe and Nick's respective cases, they could keep their money until the cows came home. Christ didn't care. God didn't either. But "Have no other gods before Me" (Exod. 20:3) is still one of God's favorite lines, and it's still one of

His rules. The rich young ruler tried to violate the rule—and as a non-believer he couldn't get into the Kingdom.

If you're a believer you may not miss heaven by having an idol or two in your life, but you'll sure put the kibosh on the Holy Spirit. Don't let money get to the top of your cone. It'll keep you chasing after the wind and have you knee-deep in footholds.

GOALS CAN BE GODS

Like money goals are driving forces in many people's lives. But it's interesting, even if people accomplish their goals, because they are driven by the goal's objectives, they are always let down. Let me illustrate.

Christmas is a biggie for me. I usually have all of my gifts purchased prior to Thanksgiving. It's true. Only I'm a softy and have a tendency to give them to my loved ones early at special appropriate moments, thereby requiring me to buy something else to put under the tree. That gets too expensive, though, so I knocked it off.

I start getting excited two weeks before Christmas day. One week before I start getting fluttery and bouncy. Two days before my breathing is rapid. The night before I'm a basket case. I don't sleep well and I fidget most of the night. And come Christmas morning, in total excitement, I tear down the stairs, rip open packages, throw ribbons, try on this, play with that and then it's time for the noon meal.

Do you know that every Christmas afternoon I can ever remember has been a downer for me? How come? Three hundred and sixty-five days to go, that's how come. I affectionately call it "postpackage depression syndrome." It's what excessive goal setting does to you. You always end up down.

I used to be quite a goal setter, but I began to notice something. If I set a goal and hit it, a period of exhilaration would be followed by a time of depression until I set another goal. If I missed the goal, I just had the depression until I set another goal. The only difference was the time of exhilaration. It's like getting anything new. The new always wears off, leaving us wanting something new again. It's postpackage depression syndrome, that's what it is. Do you know something? I never get it with Christ, but I always get it from the things of this world. Sounds like a foothold doesn't it?

Satisfaction will always be just out of reach if we pursue money or goals.

How many goals should a person accomplish in order to be able to look back on his or her life and feel good about it? Rockefeller answered the question when someone asked him, "How much money is enough?" He replied, "A little bit more than you have." Transferring that thought to goals, John D. would be telling us that we would always have to accomplish one more goal to be fulfilled. In other words, if Rocky's right (and he ought to have known), satisfaction will always be just out of reach if we pursue money or goals.

What a terrible way to have to live. It would be living like my friend Ray. Once while riding on a L.A. freeway together, he was driving much too fast. The look on his face was intense and his hands were so tight on the wheel that his knuckles turned white. I asked him, "Ray, why are you driving so fast?"

He was serious when he yelled back, "There's somebody ahead of me!"

Keeping up with the Rockefellers is an impossible goal. But trying to keep up with the Joneses is wrong goal setting too; it's godlessness. That's sin. And don't forget chronic sin produces footholds.

I don't want to live my life like that. Please don't misunderstand me. I am not putting down goal setting. Setting good goals can facilitate the proper stewardship of time, talent and treasure, but when goals become too important, or when a person's value or self-worth is dependent on what's accomplished, then goals become substitutes for God, and goal setting just becomes another form of godlessness.

When I was preparing to play for the Los Angeles Lakers, I would go to the gym and run on a treadmill. No matter how fast or slow I ran, I didn't go anyplace. It was the belt that moved. Goal setting can be like that. It feels like you're going someplace, but you don't end up any closer to God. You just get real tired. Excessive goal setting is bubbles and chasing after the wind, and it's a foothold maker.

HAPPINESS AS A GOAL IS WIND

Happiness is also a goal for most people. It's a bad one. You can't be happy all the time. If satisfaction in life is dependent upon your happiness, then you'll only be happy part of the time, and the pursuit of happiness will become your god the rest of the time. Just ask the folks who only live for the weekend.

A secular motivational speaker defined happiness as a period of time when you forget all those things that bother you. A person who thinks that way makes escapism his or her god. Drugs, alcohol, sex, projects, power, accumulation and glory all become vehicles to reach the elusive goal of continual happiness. God never intended life to be that way.

Contentment ought to be our goal, instead, and that comes through Christ. Happiness is a by-product, not an end in itself.

The apostle Paul said he was content in all his circumstances (see Phil. 4:12). He was happy in only some, but he was content in all, which showed up in his reactions to life's situations.

"We'll kill you," the Romans threatened.

"Great," Paul responded. "I'll be with the Lord."

"Since that's what you want, we won't kill you. Instead we'll beat you up and torture you." The macho men in the leather miniskirts were perplexed.

"Right on!" shouted Paul. "I'll identify with the sufferings of my Lord."

"Forget that. Okay then we'll put you in jail."

Paul was beside himself with joy as he said, "Super, every four hours I'll have a different guard chained to me. I'll share Christ with him. And in addition to that, I can get a lot of writing done."

"Since you want it we don't want to do it, so I guess we'll let you go." Now they were exasperated.

"Terrific! To live is Christ." Paul was exuberant beyond words.

What can you do to get to a person like that? Nothing! Anything! It doesn't make any difference. Paul was content in all situations. He wasn't always happy, but that great apostle was always content in Christ.

Contentment is possible when you have Christ at the top of your cone. But the pursuit of happiness will enslave you. The pursuit of happiness is bubbles and wind. It is the freeway while Christ is the narrow road. Woe to the people who get what they want when they want it.

I WANT WHAT I WANT WHEN I WANT IT

Lucy, Charlie Brown's sometimes friend and regular nemesis, says, "All I want is my fair share. All I want is what's coming to me." All she wants is everything she wants when she wants it. What would happen if that were the way life really was? How would it be if our wants and desires were always gratified?

A television series portrayed the life after death of a man who had been a gambler and chaser. He had spent his life pursuing the thrill of betting and lovin' the ladies. He awoke in a pleasant room in the presence of a well-groomed man with a beard, who was wearing a three-piece suit. The gambler thought, *This doesn't seem to be so bad,* then said, "Where am I?"

The man in the suit responded, "Home," and led the new arrival into a casino.

Our betting buddy had a quarter in his pocket and couldn't resist sticking it in a slot machine. A pull of the handle started the fruited wheels spinning, and three bars lined up in the center position. Jackpot! He hit the slot with another quarter. Jackpot again!

He was into it now. Forgetting the man in the three-piece suit, after four more jackpots the gambler put all those quarters on number 13 on the roulette table. He won! He then went to the crap table and made 20 straight passes with the dice, letting the winnings ride each time.

He was testing a theory. Can you lose in heaven? The gambler didn't think so.

Stuffing his pockets with money, he saw a beautiful woman looking at him. With a wink and a "Hey, hey," he held out his arm. She took it. There was another. Just a nod put her on the other arm and he strolled out the front door with a lovely lady on each arm, saying, "I made it, I made it. I made it to heaven. Who'd a thought it? A guy like me. I made it."

A couple of months later the gambler showed up at the casino. His eyes were deep set, hollow and dark. He had a purposeless look on his face. He was looking for the man in the three-piece suit.

After finding him the gambler made a startling statement. "Since leaving here I have not lost a hand of poker; every horse I bet on came in—win, place and show; I have called the points for every football game, not only the spread but also the totals for both teams; I always win at bingo; and I have won the lottery both times I bought a ticket. In addition every woman I want is instantly mine without the chase. I now know that in this place whatever I want will be mine whenever I want it. All dreams come true here, and quite frankly it's not for me. I'm not cut out for heaven. Not a guy like me. As a matter of fact, I would rather take my chances in hell than stay in this place. There is nothing to reach for here. There are no unknowns. Besides, I think you've made a mistake. A guy like me shouldn't be in heaven anyhow. Go ahead, send me to hell."

The dapperly dressed guide just laughed. It was a deep, guttural, belly laugh that came from the bowels of his being. And it was a profoundly evil laugh too. The gambler shuddered in waves of gooseflesh at the sound. Then the man spoke with an ironic smile, "Where do you think you are?"

Hell had been portrayed as that place where you got everything you ever wanted without the chase or the wondering of whether it would be yours. Hell was a place where you got what you wanted right when you wanted it. Lucy didn't know what she was asking for. She was asking for hell on Earth.

Would getting what you wanted when you wanted it really be so bad? It's an interesting thought. But when there is nothing left but a little bit more, there is very little to live for. One more goal, one more dollar, one more deal, one more fling, one more party or just a little more power lose their allure—but usually not until you're hooked. Not until your passion for slavery has been met. Not until you have turned away like the rich young ruler. Not until you have a well-entrenched foothold. And by that time pride and a progressively hardened heart make turning back to inquire again very difficult.

I agree with one thing for sure: If I'm going to be miserable, I'd rather be rich and miserable than poor and miserable. Wouldn't you? You bet. But why be miserable? Why not adjust your priorities, deal with your footholds and put Christ at the top? After all the rest is just chasing after the wind.

PULLING IT TOGETHER

1. Your life is like a cone and there is only room for one item on the top. If it's not Christ you've got a problem. Whenever that happens to Christians, they grieve the Spirit of God and get footholds as consequences. For unbelievers the object of greater value will keep them out of the Kingdom.

2. Money, goals, and various wants and desires are the main culprits that war with our values. We allow money to drive us, goals to frustrate us, and wants and desires to obsess us. But we do it because we think it will make us happy. A worldly focus is evidence of a foothold.

3. The pursuit of happiness is dangerous because it can become an obsessive, escalating goal. Contentment is the by-product of a right relationship with Christ. Happiness is fleeting; contentment is constant.

4. Keeping Christ at the top of our lives is the key to overcoming godlessness, but we have to be in a constant state of evaluation. Shifts can happen quickly.

HOW TO ADJUST YOUR PRIORITIES

I decided to get a train set for my kids. *It will make a great Christmas present,* I thought. I wanted the biggest and the best, so I purchased the two train packages with all the goodies and scenery.

For two weeks I drilled plywood, installed track and ran wiring. Bells belled and smoke smoked; crossing arms raised and lowered, and log cars dumped and loaded. What a layout! It would be a Christmas morning to remember.

And it was, but not as I envisioned. Oh, the kids loved the train—for about 10 minutes. It was the Vertibird helicopter from Grandpa that stole the show.

A couple of items didn't work on the train, so I used that as an excuse to take it back. Since we still needed a family toy, I used the money and got a slot car set. It was a hit. We played with it for three days.

"Buyer's remorse" is an amazing phenomenon. I got it with the train, and it hit three days after the slot cars. Before buying them I was sure they would make us happy. I was right. They did. But it didn't last.

The same thing happened with my last car. And my last DVD. And my last electronic whatchamacallit. And so on.

There is a way to deal with buyer's remorse. Solomon lived with the condition until he found out how to handle it.

Who had more money than anyone has ever had? Solomon? That's correct. He had to process some of the things we've been talking about and came to a marvelous conclusion—12 chapters after discovering his problem. It took the wisest man the world has ever seen 12 full chapters to prioritize his life. In the area of godlessness, it sometimes takes awhile to get it right. I hope you learn faster than he did. I hope I do too. In this chapter we'll learn some lessons about godlessness and buyer's remorse from King Solomon. Speak to us Daddy Big Bucks.

BEATING BUYER'S REMORSE

Solomon had it all. He went beyond anything we have ever seen. Hearst Castle is LEGOLAND in comparison to Sol's place. Kissinger's diplomatic skills pale next to Solomon's wisdom. Heff's Playboy parties are puny next to some of Solomon's bashes. Ask the Queen of Sheba about that. I'll never forget her words as she headed for home: "Sol, baby, you got class like nobody else." Those are fine words coming from a lady who knew how to "get down." Sheba was the region's number one party animal and camel-jetter. She knew what she was talkin' 'bout, and she called Solomon the best.

Solomon did everything we've ever dreamed of and more. This is what he said about his life in the book of Ecclesiastes:

I have seen all the works which have been done under the sun,
and behold, all is vanity and striving after wind (1:14).

Do you remember the definitions of "vanity of vanities" and "chasing after the wind?" "Vanity of vanities" is a bubble floating or a breath on a mirror (it looks like something's there one moment, but it's gone when you try to catch it). "Chasing after the wind" refers to the futility of trying to grab the wind. It's also called "buyer's remorse."

GRABBING FOR BUBBLES, GROPING FOR WIND

Solomon kicked off a series of specific expressions with a general statement. The paraphrased essence of his opening remarks said, "Everything the world has to offer amounts to nothing more than bubbles and wind." Have you ever seen a baby in a bathtub try to capture the personal bubbles he or she makes as they surface? It can't be done. That's what Solomon said about finding personal fulfillment from the world. It can't be done. Then he showed us what he meant:

> I said to myself, "Behold, I have magnified and increased wisdom more than all who were over Jerusalem before me; and my mind has observed a wealth of wisdom and knowledge." And I set my mind to know wisdom and to know madness and folly; I realized that this also is striving after wind (vv. 16-17).

Solomon started getting specific and began with the trait that got everything started. Smarts was his gifting from the Lord. Everything else that came his way came as the result of God's gift of excellence in the area of wisdom. But this wise one concluded that wisdom without something else amounted to nothing more than wind, which started his search for the missing something else. But what was missing?

He started sorting out the possibilities by trial and error, starting with good times:

> I said to myself, "Come now, I will test you with pleasure. So enjoy yourself." And behold, it too was futility. I said of laughter, "It is madness," and of pleasure, "What does it accomplish?" (2:1-2).

Pleasure is fun, but it's not fulfilling. Buyer's remorse happens in a hurry. Happiness is great but fleeting, and it's not contentment. It's nice to have some good times, but if that's all you live for, life is shallow. Solomon didn't find what he was looking for in pleasure.

He kept looking:

I explored with my mind how to stimulate my body with wine while my mind was guiding me wisely, and how to take hold of folly, until I could see what good there is for the sons of men to do under heaven the few years of their lives (v. 3).

Solomon tried alcohol, drugs and acting crazy. Whatever he was looking for wasn't there either.

Next he tried accumulating things:

I enlarged my works: I built houses for myself, I planted vine-yards for myself; I made gardens and parks for myself and I planted in them all kinds of fruit trees; I made ponds of water for myself from which to irrigate a forest of growing trees. I bought male and female slaves and I had homeborn slaves (vv. 4-7).

Solomon then sought fulfillment from a modified environment. He surrounded himself with things, but to no avail. He wasn't sure what was missing in his life, but it was still missing. Solomon didn't find "it" in things.

He was a persistent cuss; he didn't give up:

Also I possessed flocks and herds larger than all who preceded me in Jerusalem. Also, I collected for myself silver and gold (vv. 7-8).

Wealth, security, retirement pensions, savings, IRAs, annuities, stocks, bonds, property, jewels, rare coins and collectibles of every kind made up Solomon's portfolio. The American dream was his, but it still didn't do it for him. Now he was getting frustrated, so he went into politics:

And the treasure of kings and provinces (v. 8).

The influence, clout and political power of this potent patriarch were world-renowned. World leaders coveted his advice. His newsletter was the best circulated and most widely read publication in the civilized world. It was the *Wall Street Journal* of his time.

However, recognition and power weren't fulfilling either. There wasn't much left now. Solomon probably started wondering if he would ever find "it." *Maybe what I'm looking for is in nightlife,* so he started going out a lot:

I provided for myself male and female singers (v. 8).

"It just doesn't get any better than this" was the theme of a series of beer commercials. Solomon tried the lifestyle portrayed in the commercials and ended up hoping it would get better. He tried entertainment, sports, travel, jet-setting and good-time gatherings. He went from bashes on the beach to opening night backstage celebrations at the Met. But life's missing component still eluded the persistent aristocrat. Solomon turned to sex:

And the pleasures of men—many concubines (v. 8).

All the sex he could stand was added to what he already had and had tried. Over 1,000 women were in his household. Believe it or not contentment was still in hiding. There was one last option. Maybe there would be enough satisfaction in making a name for himself:

Then I became great and increased more than all who preceded me in Jerusalem. My wisdom also stood by me (v. 9).

Political control is one thing, but to be held in high regard is quite another. Solomon's wisdom brought him unparalleled status. Khadaffi, Khomeini and Saddam Hussein had political control, but they weren't respected. The name Kennedy has status. Mother Teresa is esteemed. Kissinger is internationally acclaimed. But no leader has ever been respected by his peers like Solomon. And yet the missing element, whatever it was, remained frustratingly out of reach.

As a last-ditch effort this baffled monarch pulled out all the stops:

> All that my eyes desired I did not refuse them. I did not withhold my heart from any pleasure (v. 10).

Solomon put the pedal to the metal; he wanted all the gusto he could get. It was time to let his hair down. Solomon decided to go for it with both barrels smokin'. He took the plunge. If there was contentment to be found in what the world had to offer, this was his last hurrah, the final fling. Open 'er up and see what she'll do. Rip and snort. Solomon tried one last time to find peace in godlessness. It was wind, and he didn't like that much, but then he didn't know what to do about it either.

FINDING "IT" IN THE WORLD

Frustrated and disappointed, that's the way Solomon felt. He chronically suffered from perpetual buyer's remorse. He couldn't find life's missing ingredient; he ran out of options. His feelings started coming through loud and clear:

> For my heart was pleased because of all my labor and this was my reward for all my labor. Thus I considered all my activities which my hands had done and the labor which I had exerted, and behold all was vanity and striving after wind and there was no profit under the sun (vv. 10-11).

There is happiness for a season in the pursuits of the world, but the chaser is always let down. There is no lasting satisfaction. Buyer's remorse always sets in. Contentment is always just out of reach. The pursuer thinks he's getting something tangible, but ends up with bubbles and wind—and maybe a few footholds too.

At least the poor still have their fantasies. The rich don't even have those. No wonder the despair is so intense, the suicide rate so high, and the alcohol and drug usage so prevalent. People who try it all have nothing to look forward to. They don't even have their dreams anymore. That is Solomon's condition:

There is happiness for a season in the pursuits of the world, but the chaser is always let down.

So I hated life, for the work which had been done under the sun was grievous to me; because everything is futility and striving after wind (v. 17).

Hear his lament. Listen to Solomon's despair. Feel the emptiness he felt. There's a foothold. Try to get into his skin for a moment. It's important to empathize with his pain or we still won't believe his conclusion to be true. When it comes to money, goals, desires and dreams, most of us are from Missouri and need to be shown. No! It's more than that. We want to see for ourselves if Solomon is wrong.

BOUNCING OFF WALLS

As adults we try to teach our kids to believe us so they won't make the same mistakes we did, and we get frustrated when they refuse to believe. They end up bouncing off the same walls we ran into. It's hard being a parent, because when our kids bounce, we bounce too. *If they would just believe us,* we secretly fret. Sometimes we verbalize it, "Please believe me, you are going to get hurt doing that." Sometimes they believe us, but usually they don't.

Are you sure this money, power and sex business is a devilish hoax? Are you kiddin'? It sounds pretty good to me. I'd sure like to try to be an exception, at least to the money and power part. Well, the money part anyhow. Is that what you're thinking?

I know. It's hard not to think that way.

God is saying, "Please believe me, you are going to get hurt doing that. You're going to bounce off a wall." But we don't believe Him. We still want the money. We still fantasize about winning the lottery. Prolonged thoughts about the rich relative leaving us an inheritance, striking oil, finding gold or whatever our daydream way of getting rich is are all evidences that we can't be trusted and that we haven't really turned that area of our lives over to God. Getting rid of it requires a "want to" coupled with a "how to." I can't help you with the "want to." You'll have to work that out yourself. The "how to" is in the next section.

REMEMBERING PBAS

I have two recommendations that will guarantee you not getting sucked into the world's trap. You can do the second one only if you decide to do the first.

First, do what Solomon did. Turn to God. Solomon's dad, King David, prayed for his son and gave him a blessing as he launched his career as king. In the midst of all the frustration, as the result of his search for contentment—the missing ingredient in his life—Solomon remembered the charge of his father:

As for you, my son Solomon, know the God of your father, and serve Him with a whole heart and a willing mind; for the LORD searches all hearts, and understands every intent of the thoughts. If you seek Him, He will let you find Him; but if you forsake Him, He will reject you forever (1 Chron. 28:9).

There it was. The answer, I mean. It hit Solomon like a ton of bricks. He had a classic "aha!" experience. He couldn't believe that he hadn't seen the forest for the trees. Seek God first. That's what Matthew would say 1,000 years later: "But seek first His kingdom and His righteousness; and all these things will be added to you" (6:33). It was an Old Testament rule and is a New Testament principle. Solomon discovered the missing ingredient, turned to God and then wrote:

> The conclusion, when all has been heard, is: fear God and keep His commandments, because this applies to every person (Eccles. 12:13).

Including wise kings—but he would only tell you that privately. It took 12 chapters and many years for Solomon to learn the lesson: Contentment is a by-product of giving everything you have, are and ever will be to God, then allowing Him to give back everything, except that which will enslave you, and trusting His decision. Footholds are the by-products of slavery to anything else.

Will you turn everything over to God and trust Him for what comes back? I hope so. You'll get HSP (Holy Spirit Power) if you do. If you don't you'll wind up with BWF (bubbles, wind and footholds).

Like his father, Solomon turned to God but he never dealt with his footholds. At the end of his life, he got deeply involved with the wrong kind of ladies and as a result didn't finish life well. The world system can do that to you if you let it.

Second, and dependent upon the first, take worldly thoughts captive to the obedience of Christ. That's right, have PBAs (polar bear alerts) as often as you recognize your fantasies moving toward things, bucks, clout and the rest. Practice the concept of PBAs and you'll experience some incredible victories over the world system.

The world system appeals to our sin nature. Glitter, bubbles and wind have a strong attraction to Adam's flesh. Without keeping the old man in check, we will succumb to the things of this earth. That's why the concept of a polar bear alert is so important. Our biggest obstacle in overcoming the world's system is overcoming ourselves. Therefore, we have to be constantly on the alert to see if our priorities have changed. Things can hop up on top of our cone quickly and unexpectedly.

Priority shifts happen all the time and can be confusing because we rarely know they're changing until they've changed. Sometimes we don't even know they've changed. For example, Peter thought Jesus' neck was more important than Malchus's ear one minute, but considered his own hide more valuable than his Lord's skin the next three times in a row. As a matter of fact, all the disciples thought more of their skins than Christ's until the Holy Spirit countered their sin natures.

Ask God about any priority changes that have occurred in your life. Sincerely ask the Holy Spirit to search your heart. He'll be faithful if you don't have any éclairs hidden in your refrigerator.

Are you ready to check your priorities? Have you checked your heart? Failure to check your heart before you check your priorities can be disastrous, even fatal. Ask Ananias and Sapphira about that. They had some serious heart trouble, as we'll see in the next chapter.

PULLING IT TOGETHER

1. Polar bear alerts are the key to controlling worldly thoughts. Remember, you have a sin nature, you have to endure direct fiery darts from the enemy and you live under the world's system. That's three contact points. Of course you will have ungodly thoughts, but polar bear alerts can bring them under control.

2. Also, remember the slavery concept. You were made to be a slave, so choose God as your master, not the things of the world. While God's enslavement will set you free, the world's enslavement is pure bondage and produces footholds.

3. Priority shifts happen in a hurry. Be in a constant state of evaluating the positioning of Christ on your cone. Keep Him at the top. You'll have to search your heart to do that. Control the éclairs and don't fool yourself or try to fool God. Trying to snooker God is especially dangerous.

The following illustration is not a slam on multilevel marketing organizations. Every field has a few bad eggs. I was tired of portraying used car dealers and life insurance salespeople as bad guys—they need a break—so I chose a fictitious company called "ShackWayLife." (Now nobody will get mad—I hope.)

Ananias and Sapphira were at the "All-State" level with Shack WayLife and enjoyed being in a big church because of all the contacts available to them. They liked Peter's church because it was growing so fast. "Exploding" would be a better word. It seemed as if thousands were added every time he opened his mouth. In fact, 3,000 to 5,000 at a time.

While Sapphira prepared for their evening recruiting presentations, Ananias did a little land developing on the side, making it easier to reply what he did for a living when people asked. (They didn't want to tell new prospects what they did for a living until they got them to an opportunity meeting, so the development business was a good cover.)

With all the new folks in church, the church needed to raise money for a bigger sanctuary and more Christian education space. Most of the church folk caught the vision and started bringing everything they had for the Lord's work.

Not wanting to be outdone (it would be bad for business), Ananias and Sapphira sold a piece of property, brought part of the money and gave it to the elders. The problem occurred when the couple said they had given the total proceeds from the sale, when actually they had only given a portion.

God didn't really care if they gave all, part or none of the proceeds from the sale. What He did care about was lying—He cared about why they lied and the reason they gave. This godless couple didn't care about God; they cared about business. They didn't care about the Kingdom; they cared about appearances. They didn't care about ministry; they cared about feathering their nest.

Attitudes like that are footholds for the devil. God told Peter what they had done and Peter told them—in spades.

Peter sent for Ananias. Before going to see Peter, Ananias, whose office was close to the church, called Sapphira and excitedly said, "Peter has called us to the church. I think he's impressed by our gift, and he'll probably endorse us in front of the Body this Sunday [actually it was Saturday, but you know what I mean—don't be picky]. Selling that land, giving a piece of the profits and telling the church it was the total amount was the best business decision we could ever have made. We'll be at 'All-American' before we know it. Pretty soon we may even start doing motivational tapes for the company and speaking at rallies. 'All-World' level here we come. I'm going over to the church to see 'Pete' right now. Come as soon as you can."

Sapphira was so excited, but in her haste she failed to gas the car. It ran out of fuel on the freeway. Sapphira called AAA. Ananias went straight to the church for the news.

He was pleased when he walked in. All the elders were present, along with Peter. *They're probably going to lay hands on me,* Ananias thought as he entered the room. *I'm finally in the inner circle.* His thoughts turned to

Matthew. *I'll bet he's about ready to attend a ShackWayLife meeting. He's had a little taste of money in his day. I'll bet he's ready to have a taste again. With his contacts he could become a "Direct" in no time.*

With growing horror Ananias listened to Peter. The tone of his voice spelled trouble:

Ananias, why has Satan filled your heart [that's a foothold] to lie to the Holy Spirit and to keep back some of the price of the land? While it remained unsold, did it not remain your own? And after it was sold, was it not under your control? Why is it that you have conceived this deed in your heart? You have not lied to men but to God (Acts 5:3-4).

Peter finished speaking, and before Ananias could start smooth talking, God snuffed him. Just like that. He had a massive coronary, right there, right then. Do you think that didn't put the fear of God into the bystanders? It freaked them out to the max. They all wondered if they had told any lies to God lately and looked over their shoulders for lightning bolts.

Peter didn't waste any time burying Ananias. It was done before his wife arrived. Ananias had been right about the elders laying hands on him—but they did so to plant him, not bless him.

Sapphira was three hours late and a bit perturbed at the auto club for taking their sweet time. But she greeted everyone cheerfully and smiled inside at the turnout. *This was going to be better than I thought.* Ananias had thought the same thing when he'd walked in. Devious minds travel in the same gutter.

Sapphira didn't even get to give a special greeting to Matthew. She'd talked to Ananias about zeroing in on him; this lady was all business. She was just beginning to wonder why her husband wasn't there when Peter spoke sternly, "Tell me whether you sold the land for 20,000 dollars?"

The news traveled fast, she thought and was pleased the prayer chain had worked so quickly. Forgetting about her husband she quickly responded, "Yes, that's right. I'm sure it's the biggest gift you've received, and yes, it's sure okay with us if you put a gold plaque in the foyer of the new sanctuary in our honor." She thought that might be very good for business and was pleased with herself for being so quick to think of it.

Then Peter said to her, "Why is it that you have agreed together to put the Spirit of the Lord to the test? Behold, the feet of those who have buried your husband are at the door, and they will carry you out as well" (v. 9).

Déjà vu. Like her husband Sapphira dropped before a peep came out of her mouth. The only difference was that God ruptured her aorta instead of giving her the coronary He'd given Ananias. The result was the same, though actually a little quicker.

Word of the two deaths traveled fast on the prayer chain. Everyone realized just how serious God was about whom or what owned their hearts, and they concluded that it was dumb to try and snow Him. Not even becoming an "All-Universe" was worth the risk.

God is just as serious today as He was then about having pure hearts. So don't make the mistake of trying to pull the wool over God's eyes or be double-minded with Him. It can't be done. If you try there is a price to pay. Remember, He knows your innermost secrets and motivations. You'll never hide from it or get away with it.

Ananias and Sapphira allowed their love for the world system to progress to the point of allowing Satan's influence to focus on them. They allowed footholds to develop, and they never checked their hearts to see if they lost ground to the enemy.

TAKE AN EKG (HOW'S YOUR HEART?)

How is your heart?

Is it pure before God? Do you want God to search it?

If so pray through the following psalms. This is your last time in prayer. *Don't shortcut the process.* These prayers are just as important as the others—and you've come so far. Finish properly. Remember, pray out loud and with authority.

PRAYER

O LORD, you have examined my heart and know everything about me. You know when I sit down or stand up. You know my every thought when far away. You chart the path ahead of me and tell me where to stop and rest. Every moment you know where I am. You know what I am going to say even before I say it, LORD. You both precede and follow me. You place your hand of blessing on my head. Such knowledge is too wonderful for me, too great for me to know! I can never escape from your spirit! I can never get away from your presence! If I go up to heaven, you are there; if I go down to the place of the dead, you are there. If I ride the wings of the morning, if I dwell by the farthest oceans, even there your hand will guide me, and your strength will support me. I could ask the darkness to hide me and the light around me to become night—but even in darkness I cannot hide from you. To you the night shines as bright as day. Darkness and light are both alike to you. You made all the delicate, inner parts of my body and knit me together in my mother's womb. Thank you for making me so wonderfully complex! Your workmanship is marvelous—and how well I know it. You watched me as I was being formed in utter seclusion, as I was woven together in the dark of the womb. You saw me before I was born. Every day of my life was recorded in your book. Every moment was laid out before a single day had passed. Search me, O God, and know my heart; test me and know my thoughts. Point out anything in me that offends you, and lead me along the path of everlasting life (Ps. 139:1-16,23-24, NLT).

Do you really want God to search you and test you, to bring your ways into alignment with His ways? Do you want Him to help you change what's harmful in your life? Are you willing to change your hurtful ways?

Do you want to live life your way or God's way? Be honest about your conclusion. David's psalm of repentance may help you make up your mind. Pray through it.

PRAYER

Have mercy on me, O God, because of your unfailing love. Because of your great compassion, blot out the stain of my sins. Wash me clean from my guilt. Purify me from my sin. For I recognize my shameful deeds—they haunt me day and night. Against you, and you alone, have I sinned; I have done what is evil in your sight. You will be proved right in what you say, and your judgment against me is just. For I was born a sinner—yes, from the moment my mother conceived me. But you desire honesty from the heart, so you can teach me to be wise in my inmost being. Purify me from my sins, and I will be clean; wash me, and I will be whiter than snow. Oh, give me back my joy again; you have broken me—now let me rejoice. Don't keep looking at my sins. Remove the stain of my guilt. Create in me a clean heart, O God. Renew a right spirit within me. Do not banish me from your presence, and don't take your Holy Spirit from me. Restore to me again the joy of your salvation, and make me willing to obey you. Then I will teach your ways to sinners, and they will return to you. Forgive me for shedding blood, O God who saves; then I will joyfully sing of your forgiveness. Unseal my lips, O Lord, that I may praise you. You would not be pleased with sacrifices, or I would bring them. If I brought you a burnt offering, you would not accept it. The sacrifice you want is a broken spirit. A broken and repentant heart, O God, you will not despise (Ps. 51:1-17, NLT).

Is it your desire to have a broken spirit and to place yourself under the authority of God? Do you understand God wants your willing heart more than He wants anything else from you? Service, ministry, Bible study or prayer will not take the place of a broken heart. Be sure you understand that concept.

As we take on the devil's henchmen, who are in charge of this world and its system, there is a very important passage of Scripture to discuss. An understanding of and faith in this portion of God's Word will ensure your victory in overcoming improper priorities:

This is the way to find out if they have the Spirit of God: If a prophet acknowledges that Jesus Christ became a human being, that person has the Spirit of God. If a prophet does not acknowledge Jesus, that person is not from God. Such a person has the spirit of the Antichrist. You have heard that he is going to come into the world, and he is already here.

But you belong to God, my dear children. You have already won your fight with these false prophets, because the Spirit who lives in you is greater than the spirit who lives in the world. These people belong to this world, so they speak from the world's viewpoint, and the world listens to them. But we belong to God; that is why those who know God listen to us. If they do not belong to God, they do not listen to us. That is how we know if someone has the Spirit of truth or the spirit of deception (1 John 4:2-6, *NLT*).

Do you understand? God in you, in the form of the Holy Spirit, is stronger than the devil and the world system. The Father promises to sort out your priorities if you sincerely want Him to, but you have to be willing to alter them if He demonstrates the need.

BREAKING FOOTHOLDS

It's now time to go to war.

I'll list topics for prayer. You'll be praying about those areas that were problems for Solomon as well as some others I'll bring up. As you pray you'll find yourself going off on tangents, as one subject may cause you to think of another. That's okay. Let the Lord take you wherever He wants to take you.

PRAYER

Almighty God in heaven I come to You now asking You to show me if my priorities are wrong. Demonstrate to me if my emphasis on the things of this world is proper and pleasing to You. I will trust You to do that now as I follow Solomon's list of worldly pursuits.

Pleasure. Father, do I live for pleasure? Is the pursuit of happiness too important to me? Am I more interested in me than I am in You? Am I seeking fulfillment in life through self-gratification rather than glorifying You?

Laughter. Do I have a party spirit, Lord? Do I want to escape life's responsibilities and a deeper relationship with You by substituting shallowness? Am I attempting to run from You by not getting serious enough? Lord God, am I too casual about hell and the impact Satan has on Your children? Do I not understand the value of a soul? Show me if I need to reassess my values.

Substances. What do You want me to do about drinking? Is it okay? When? How much, Lord? Some? None? Do alcohol or drugs play too great a role in my life? Am I hooked on something but don't realize it? Is my growing dependence showing up by hurt relationships or harm to the members of my family? Has my problem gone so far that I need some help in overcoming it?

Folly. Have I gone the way of the fool, Lord? Have I failed to seek counsel; have I rejected the advice of Your messengers? Have I been too intent on having my way, instead of Your way? Is authority a problem for me? Do I hide from responsibility You intend for me to have?

Things. Have I put more trust in things than I have in You, almighty God? Am I too caught up in acquiring? Are properties, comforts and amenities more important to me than You? Are the treasures of this earth keeping me from serving you according to Your will?

Wealth. Heavenly Father, with all my heart I desire to know if money is too important to me. It appears to be one of life's greatest and most common stumbling blocks. Is it a stumbling block for me? Am I more concerned about my retirement than You or making that payment or saving? Have I allowed money to come between us?

Political Control. Father, do I desire power over people more than I desire to be obedient to You? Is my desire for dominance greater than my passion to glorify You? Is my drive up the corporate ladder in proper perspective? Does teaching my Sunday School class mean too much to me? Am I on that committee for the right reason?

Status. Lord, do I let how people feel toward me mean more than it ought? Do I care more about what they say about me than what they say about You? Does my value and self-worth come more from my position in life and how others esteem me than it does from understanding how much You value me? Do I want into or out of a job too badly?

*Almighty God and heavenly Father, I tire of trying to find
meaning in life apart from You. Life is not to be spent with You on
the sidelines. That I might be content in You and accept that measure
of happiness that is to be my portion is my deepest desire.
Father, thank You for taking back the ground I gave to the devil.
I come to You now as my deliverer from Satan's kingdom of darkness
and his dominion of bondage with all its miseries. I claim the promise of
Your Word that whoever calls on the name of the Lord shall be delivered
and set free. I call upon You now. For the victory I give You honor,
praise and thanksgiving. You are a faithful, amazingly awesome God.
I am so grateful for what You have done for me today. I am free, and
I praise Your holy name. I thank You in Jesus' name, amen.*

Congratulations!

You did it. You submitted to God, prayed, resisted and won. The counterattack has been completed. You are now on the offensive.

If for some reason you've failed to pray the prayers that are presented in this book, why not go back and fight the battle for your lost ground properly? All believers are forgiven, but not all are free.

Let me tell you one more story.

I had finished speaking one evening during a summer camp when a counselor stopped to talk to me. In her mid-40s the lady knew her Bible well. She had a small tattoo on her shoulder. I was captivated by what she told me.

She had gone to a counselor to seek help for a problem. She didn't know it, but the counselor had a drug habit. He counseled her into becoming dependent on him, hooked her on drugs and then turned her to the streets as a prostitute to support them both. As it turned out she fell in love with her pimp, he fell in love with her, they got married and years later ended up getting saved.

Here she was, several years after receiving Christ, counseling high school girls. But things weren't quite right. The messages were bringing up problems she hadn't dealt with. Footholds! Years of sex, drugs and rebellion make for lots of leeches. Her swim in the swamp had made room for aliens. She had been forgiven, but there was old ground that needed to be taken back.

Each night after the meetings, she went through the prayers presented in this book. The result? She went home changed. She came to camp forgiven, but she went home free.

I pray that you are just as free as she is. You can be.

DEBRIEFING: FIX YOUR PENCIL, MAINTAIN YOUR MENISCUS

I was sitting with a dear friend, enjoying a soda and talking theology. (As much as I can talk about it anyhow. Remember, I'm a layman and haven't been to Bible school.) I'll not identify my friend because he didn't want anyone to think he was being blasphemous. He took a pencil, broke it and as he handed the pieces to me said, "Pretend I'm God for a moment." Handing me the broken pencil he continued, "Here, take care of this pencil. Make sure it doesn't get broken."

I don't understand why I have to suffer because Adam blew it, and I don't understand why the sins of the father are visited on generations of kids. But I guess I don't have to understand. I don't understand much about electricity; however, it works whether I understand it or not. And I was born with a sin nature whether I understand much about it or not. It too works regardless of my understanding.

Although I inherited a pencil that has already been broken, I can piece it back together. As a matter of fact I'm supposed to work toward fixing it. But the repairs cannot be done alone. I need to enlist the help of the Holy Spirit, because fixing the damage is tough and can be a real battle sometimes.

We will not fix the crack in the pencil in our lifetime. We can progressively get more and more of the pieces back in place, but the powers of hell will continue to exert themselves, added pressure from the continual battle of our innermost parts will continue to rage and temptations resulting from trying to live in the world system without becoming a part of it will continue to flare-up. Those combined forces will produce enough tension to keep the crack in the pencil from ever being repaired this side of glory. And the same pressures are constantly present to break the pencil if we ever relax our will and grieve or quench the power of the Holy Spirit in our lives by sinning. When that happens we have to start piecing the pencil back together again.

We can start with forgiveness of sin through Jesus Christ and the energizing power of the Holy Spirit. Submission to God's authority is a major facilitator for repair. Warfare prayer and the removal of footholds help put the remaining loose pieces in place and bring the two broken ends together. But only with our glorified bodies will the crack be removed. Until that occurs it's our job to properly refit the pieces and keep the two ends together.

The best way I know to keep the pencil together is to train yourself to have progressively faster polar bear alerts whenever temptation occurs (see 2 Cor. 10:5). That will lengthen your time between stumbles. Then, when you do sin, confess it faster so that time spent without the power of the Holy Spirit is minimized (see 1 John 1:9). Let me illustrate with a glass of water.

MAINTAIN YOUR MENISCUS

In my right hand visualize a clear drinking glass. In my left hand visualize a pitcher of water. I'm pouring some water into the glass while slowly lowering the glass, making the stream of water as long as I can. When the water is a quarter of an inch from the top, I stop pouring.

The glass represents your life. The water is the Holy Spirit. (No illustration is ever quite complete. This is not an exception to the rule, because no matter how much water is in the glass, it is still 100 percent of the Holy Spirit. He is an entity and is referred to as the person of the Holy Spirit. You can't get half of Him or any part of Him for that matter. You either got Him or you don't got Him. That's terrible English, but it's great theology. Regardless of how much water is in the glass, it still represents all of the Holy Spirit.)

Look carefully at the lip of the glass and visualize an oil spout squirting dirty motor oil. That's your sin nature, and it is always pumping; it never stops.

If the water is a quarter of an inch from the top, what's filling up the rest of the glass? Is oil lighter or heavier than water? Lighter, that's correct. So will it settle to the bottom of the glass or stay at the top? Right again, it will fill the space at the top. But what happens to the oil when I slowly pour water into the glass? Yes, the oil runs down the side of the glass.

Water has a surface tension. It's the tension that forms water into drops. The tension adheres to the roughness on the side of the glass, forming a little umbrella shape. It's called a meniscus. And if I pour carefully, I can actually get more water in the glass than there is glass. Where has the oil gone that was in the glass? Down the side. And where is the oil going that is still squirting out of the spout? Down the side. There is no room in the glass; it's full. That's what Ephesians 5:18 means when it says that we are to "be filled with the Spirit."

In the Greek the word "filled" means a continual filling, not a one-time occurrence. Since we will always have a sin nature, and since we never fully defeat it (at best we can only control it), we have to stay full, not just get filled.

I have been sealed with the Holy Spirit of promise (see Eph. 1:13). That happens—once—when a person receives Jesus Christ as Savior. But I will need to be filled as often as I grieve and quench the Spirit through sin. In other words, staying filled requires lifelong attention. When I sin

I slosh some of the water out of the glass. What fills up the new space? Oil, of course. And if I don't do anything about it, I'll sin again, sloshing out more water, and again and again. And then I'll commit a really big sin, which almost empties the glass of water and makes room for a lot of oil. It's interesting that as water comes out, oil comes out too and gets all over me, and it gets all over anyone who happens to be near me. Sin is messy for me and for those close to me.

What's the solution?

A spiritual person can't stand not being full.

If we confess our sins, He is faithful and righteous to forgive us our sins and to cleanse us from all unrighteousness (1 John 1:9).

Visualize water slowly being poured in up to the very top and just beyond. I am filled when there is no room for oil. First John 1:9 does that for me.

Never am I almost full. I am either full or I'm not. Most people would look at a glass with a sixteenth of an inch of room at the top and call it filled ("almost anyway" or "close enough"). That's because they look from the side. God doesn't look at things the way I do. He looks down from the top. And in a glass that's not quite full of water what will He see from that angle? A thin layer of oil—not full! That person is badly in need of a 1 John 1:9 confession treatment.

People who slosh but fill right up with 1 John 1:9 don't slosh as much water out, and they don't slosh as often. As a matter of fact, a good measure of their love for the Lord is whether they lengthen their time between sloshes, and if when they do slosh, they decrease the time it takes to fill back up. A spiritual person can't stand not being full.

Actually, a person who loves God enjoys life the most when a little trickle of water is constantly flowing into the glass. Sometimes I can do that for a week or two. Some of my friends do it a little longer. But then I travel with a rough crowd and can lose the trickle.

Lengthen your time between stumbles and decrease the amount of time before confession. That's the mark of a spiritual person. And don't worry about the crack in the pencil. Just keep the pieces together. You can do that by maintaining your meniscus.

Finally, don't worry about footholds resulting from a mess-up. One mess-up does not a foothold make.

DON'T WORRY IF YOU MESS UP

Satan doesn't rush into a life. His demonic host oozes in. One sin is not an opening for him unless it goes unconfessed. Unconfessed sin over a period of time and repeated sin create opportunities for the enemy. Therefore, lengthening time between stumbles and decreasing time before confession is the best way I know of to keep footholds from establishing or reestablishing.

If you mess up royally and allow the enemy another beachhead, then go through the warfare prayers again. Do it as often as necessary. *And by the way, if you skipped over the prayers in order to read the meat of the book, the meat was in the part you skipped.* Why not intently go through the prayers in chapters 5, 10 and 13?

SOME SERIOUS COUNSEL

If going through these procedures seems to uncover and stir up darkness, and it doesn't lift or clear, you may need to seek out a pastor or counselor experienced in deliverance ministry to pray further with you, especially if you've been involved in the occult, incest, or deep hatred and bitterness by you or others close to you. These things sometimes result in heavier strongholds that need to be broken by added discernment or authority. This book is designed to help you through "deliverance the easy way." If the prayers stir up some hard stuff and you need help, seek it out. Don't be afraid if you realize you need it.

Remember, fear is from your enemy. Resist it while you seek additional help.

LET WAR GO ON

War may continue to rage in your inner nature for a season. Don't be concerned if things are a little disrupted for a few days. As Jesus told the disciples, some deliverance takes prayer and fasting (see Matt. 17:19-21; Mark 9:28-29). Well, freedom from footholds sometimes takes extra time too. Let the warring angels of God do their thing. And don't worry they'll do a complete job. However, just because you thumped the devil's rump once doesn't mean he won't come at you again.

Satan had to leave Christ in the wilderness on command, but that didn't keep him away (see Matt. 4:10-11). That dragon returned when Christ's humanity was exposed in the garden scene prior to the cross. In other words, commanding the enemy in the name of Christ is like putting a child to bed. You may put your two-year-old in bed, but that doesn't necessarily mean he or she will stay there. Just as Satan returned to harass Jesus at His moment of weakness, he is there again when your humanity is exposed. And sometimes you lose battles because you trust in your humanness instead of God's omnipotence. After a loss it's a good idea to check for footholds, so don't put this book too far away. Use the prayer sections occasionally to see how you're doing.

You now know how to do that. Start by prayerfully asking yourself some questions under the guidance of the Holy Spirit:

1. Who am I mad at? Have I dealt with some anger improperly? Do I harbor a root of bitterness?
2. Has any sexual sin crept into my life? Fantasy? Lingering looks? Prolonged wishes? Messing with variables? Overt sin?

3. Is there any form of godlessness going on in my life? Have God do a priority check on you. Check your cone to see what's on top.

If God shows you something, 1 John 1:9-it with a repentant heart. Do that quickly. Remember, éclairs in your refrigerator kill the power of prayer and keep the Holy Spirit grieved and quenched, just like any other sin does, so make sure your heart's right.

As soon as you've applied 1 John 1:9, purpose to lengthen your time between stumbles. Do that by applying 2 Corinthians 10:5 and having a polar bear alert. That's the only way I know to keep from sinning, and it's worth one more reminder to help you learn to do it. The effective usage of 1 John 1:9 and 2 Corinthians 10:5 prevents footholds.

A PERSONAL NOTE

This book has been an attempt to match the practical with the academic. I wanted it to have enough scholarship to be credible, but I also wanted it to be practical. You probably noticed that I wanted the book to be fun too. I hope you were able to smile in between dealing with the hard stuff.

I put out a monthly online newsletter called *eThots*. I'd be honored to have you on the list. Go to www.jaycarty.com to sign up.

It has been a pleasure serving you.

Helping drain the swamp for Jesus,
Jay Carty

PS Stay out of the swamp until it's drained.

APPENDIX

FOR COUPLES WHO COUPLED TOO SOON

If you are a woman, try to get your husband to read this book. Then see if he would lead in the following prayer. Remember 1 Peter 3:1. Your behavior will go a lot further in bringing a disobedient man into a right relationship with God than your words will. It is hard for a woman to "gum" her husband into the Kingdom. Men don't usually respond well to it.

If you are a man, and you sense the bitterness toward your bride that I'm talking about, have her read this book so you will be on the same wavelength spiritually. Then get alone together, preferably in bed, since that's where the original violation took place, hold each other and pray a warfare prayer rebuking the enemy of bitterness assigned to you. Take the past ground back verbally. Fully repent. Resist the devil. And then ask God to begin to restore the years that the locusts have eaten (see Joel 2:25). If you pray together you may find your bitterness leave and a wonderful restoration take place between you.

The following is an example of the kind of prayer I'm suggesting:

Heavenly Father, my wife and I come before You tonight with a desire to make sure that old wrongs are set right and to drive away the influence that was assigned to us by our enemy after our sin. Our desire is to confess our sin and fully repent before You, and to resist the devil in the authority of Jesus Christ in order to take back the ground we gave through our wrongdoing. Father, we come before You in the name that is above all names, Jesus Christ. Lord, we are before You together to confess the sin of our mutual premarital sexual encounter(s). We were foolish, prideful, lustful and wrong. It was evil in Your sight. We're sorry, we're repentant and like David we would ask that You create new hearts in us. Thank You for the privilege of confession and thank You for the gift of forgiveness.

Thank You for choosing to remember our sin no more. We also want to come against the enemies of Christ that were assigned to harass us because of the ground we gave to the devil through sexual sin. We reclaim that ground in the power of Jesus Christ and we come against the bitterness that resulted between us as partners in marriage. Satan, we know what you are about and we claim the power of our resurrected Lord. Father in heaven, remove the foothold and the influence the enemy has had over us. Thank You, Lord, for allowing us to be more than conquerors. And thank You for this victory. In Jesus' name, amen.

A STUDY GUIDE FOR
BASIC TRAINING FOR SPIRITUAL COMBAT

By Sam Talbert (Jay's Paul)

INTRODUCTION

Some books should be read and enjoyed, some should be read and understood, and some others should not be read at all. This book should be both enjoyed and understood. It is a delight to read and I will guarantee that you will be entertained as you read it. However, if you stop there you will miss the real intention the author had in mind for writing it. There is a message of great importance to be gained here. We don't want you to miss the truths that are unfolding here. Therefore, we offer these pages to you as our attempt to help you understand.

This book is intended to be a study guide and that presupposes a couple of things. First of all, we assume that you want to "study" the subject of this book. If you just wanted to read about this subject, you wouldn't be looking at this study guide. Knowing this helps us determine the approach we want to take in developing this guide. Second, we can assume that you are willing to be "guided" through the material in the book.

We make no assumption that this will be the first time that you have read this book. Having read the book, you have found already some valuable information for your walk with God. However, there is a dimension that we will offer to you in this study guide that will further enhance the impact this book has already had in your life.

We also are looking at the probability that this study guide will be used as a resource for small Bible study groups, support groups and the like. Therefore, we have taken an approach that will make this guide a valuable tool in leading a small group discussion on this material.

Now, a word about the format of this study guide. We are dividing the material into three phases. These three approaches are as follows:

ON MY OWN

This section is specifically targeted at individuals who are working by themselves, either to study the material on their own or to prepare to participate in the discussion when his or her group comes together. In this section there will be guided reading assignments wherein you will be directed to read the chapters, looking for specific concepts, or specific answers to questions. This approach may adjust your reading habits and that is a part of our goal. We want to help you to read better, faster, and more insightfully. Hopefully, you will learn some principles that will transfer to other books and studies, and enable you to read more and get more out of what you read. Don't misunderstand, we are not trying to duplicate Evelyn Woods, but there are some basic techniques that are easily learned and when put into practice, make a significant difference in your comprehension.

We will also send you to the Word of God to look at the passages that undergird the principles that are taught in this book. In this section we will be encouraging you to look carefully at the text and make observations about what you find there. Questions like: "Who is this about?" "What is happening here?" "Where did this take place?" "What is the time frame here?" "How did he do that?" In short, we will be encouraging you to collect data from the Scriptures that will help you to understand the principles that are laid out in the book you are studying.

We will also send you into the book to find the principles and ideas that are expounded there. Our goal is to guide you to arrive at the principles that Jay is teaching in somewhat the same manner that he did. By looking into the scripture and following his line of reasoning you will thoroughly understand the principles he is teaching.

DISCUSSION QUESTIONS

In this section you will find three kinds of questions. First, there will be those questions that open the subject of the chapter to discussion designed to focus our attention on that subject. Second, there will be questions that center around the principles that have been derived from the personal research "On My Own." This is important for two reasons. We want to affirm those who took the time to do the work beforehand, and we want to avoid the "pooling of ignorance." We are interested in the principles that have been carefully extracted from the Scripture. Third, there are questions that lead us to application. We are interested in life change and have no interest in filling your head with more useless facts. If we cannot stimulate you to apply these truths, then we have failed in our most important objective.

NOTES FOR GROUP LEADERS

In this section we will talk to those who take on the responsibility of facilitating a group. These people who accept the challenge of becoming an agent of God in the lives of a small group are the backbone of the church and its ministry. Too many churches have the misguided concept that the preacher will do it. "After all, that is why we hired him, isn't it?" Unfortunately, there are not enough churches that understand that you did not hire the preacher to "do it." You hired him to train you so that you can "do it." Therefore, to you who step forward and take the challenge of being a small-group leader, we say, "Praise God for you and may your tribe increase!" We want to do everything we can to help you be a success in your venture of ministering to your small group.

Our concept is this: Jay wrote this book out of his own study and experiences, and he has a desire to lead each person to the application of the book. However, he is not available to come to your group and make the application, as much as he would like to. So, we want to train you, the small-group leader, to take Jay's place and stand for him in making the application.

BASIC TRAINING FOR SPIRITUAL COMBAT
TAKING BACK THE HIGH GROUND

ON MY OWN

Before we dive into the book we want you to take a look at the table of contents. You will notice that there are three "Warfare" sections. These tell us that Jay has organized his book around some introductory thoughts and three main topics. List the three topics below:

1.

2.

3.

Also, while we are looking at the table of contents, there is something interesting about chapters 5, 10 and 13. What did you notice about these chapters?

These chapters are the applications for all that Jay has in mind in this book. Without these chapters this book is just another intellectual exercise about which we could easily yawn and say, "That's interesting." The enemy would like nothing better. When we get to these chapters we wills top and apply the truths we have learned, and use this book as the tool for righteousness that it was intended to be.

Now let's go back to the beginning of the book.

The first few pages are nice but have little to do with the meat of the book. However, you should read them if for no other reason than to note that my name appears there. You should also read the Boston Gardens story. It sets the tone for the book and it is a great story. You will enjoy it. Now, for chapter 1.

CHAPTER 1
CRUCIAL CONCEPTS FOR WAR

ON MY OWN

Wait, don't start reading yet. Turn to the end of any chapter and look at the section called "Pulling It Together." That section gives you a summary of what was in the chapters. I know this is cheating. But, if you want to get the gist of what the chapter is all about you can quickly go to this section at the end of each chapter, and *bingo*! There is all of the meat of the chapter without all of the gravy.

Now that we know the chapter is all about Éclairs, Polar Bears, Footholds, and Double-mindedness, we know what to look for as we read. OK, now you can start reading. When you finish chapter 1, I will have some questions for you.

DISCUSSION QUESTIONS FOR CHAPTER 1

1. What is the significance of the story of the Vietnamese pig?
2. What does May mean by the concept of "Éclairs in Your Refrigerator"?
3. What do you think, when does temptation become sin?
4. Explain how the "Polar Bear Alert" works.
5. What causes footholds for the enemy?
6. Memorize 2 Corinthians 10:5.

NOTES FOR GROUP LEADERS

The Boston Gardens story is a good chapter to get the flavor of the book. You may want to spend some time talking about this chapter just to get to know the people in your group. Even women will enjoy the story though they may not be interested in basketball.

Be sure to call attention to chapters 5, 10, and 13. These chapters are what make this book different from any other book. Truth proclaimed but not applied is worth than worthless, it is dangerous. It is a subtle suggestion that God really doesn't mean what He says, Christianity is just a game, and it really doesn't matter. You and I both know that it really *does* matter, and God help us if we handle lightly what God is dead serious about.

Chapter 1 is an important chapter that forms a basis for the following sections. It is important for the group to understand the concept of double-mindedness. Without getting a handle on this they will be powerless and frustrated throughout the remainder of the book. Remember, *when your imagination comes in conflict with your will, your imagination usually wins.*

The main points you want them to go away with are:

1. We are in a war whether we know it or not.
2. Double-minded prayers are powerless.
3. Substitute-thinking works.
4. Lingering in sin complicates freedom.

Assign the memorization of 2 Corinthians 10:5 as a homework assignment.

WARFARE ON FOOTHOLD #1

The next three chapters are going to deal with one major subject: Anger. Let's take them one at a time.

CHAPTER 2
HOW MAD ARE YOU?

ON MY OWN

Wait. Hold it. Don't start reading yet. Turn to the "Pulling It Together" section for chapter 2. Let's take a peek at what Jay thinks is important in this chapter. Answer these questions:

1. What four emotions generally precede anger?
2. Is anger sin?
3. Why is anger dangerous?

Now you are ready to read the chapter. (For you advanced students, Jay used a word picture that is interesting. Look for the word "worm sweat" and be prepared to discuss its usage in the context.)

Jay relates four stories which illustrate emotions leading to anger. List the emotion connected with each story:

Physical and Emotional "Ouchies" –

"Yikes" and "Whillikers" —

What Kind of "Bleep" Is This? –

It's Not Fair –

(For you advanced students, who is the youth pastor?)

Jay mentions two passages of Scripture from the book of Ephesians. Highlight those references and go to your Bible and read the whole of chapter 4. It is only 32 verses and it will help you when we discuss it in our group.

In the "Anger Progression" section, Jay defines each of the words in Ephesians 4:31. List his definitions below:

Bitterness –

Wrath –

Anger –

Clamor –

Slander –

Malice –

In the "Termites of Bitterness" section, what is the only real reason to forgive someone?

DISCUSSION QUESTIONS FOR CHAPTER 2

1. Share the last time you remember getting angry, and determine the emotions that preceded your anger.
2. Is anger a sin? Why? Or why not?
3. In a situation where anger occurs, when it is sin, if at all?
4. How do you resolve the apparent contradiction between Ephesians 4:26 where we are told to "be angry and sin not" and Ephesians 4:31 where we are told to "put away...anger"?
5. In a dictionary look up the words found in Ephesians 4:31.
6. If there is only one legitimate reason to forgive someone, what is it? What happens when we introduce other reasons for forgiving someone?
7. What is "worm sweat"?

NOTES FOR GROUP LEADERS

Start with Jay's instruction, on page 29, to stop and remember the last time they were angry. Encourage each person in the group to share and discuss the emotions that preceded each episode of anger. Discuss the stories that Jay tells and let the group relate to them, asking, "Which of the situations most often pops up in your life?"

You want your group to understand that there are some emotions that generally always precede anger. Also, make sure that everyone understands the truth that anger is not a sin. Anger is a symptom that something is wrong and needs to be corrected. It's an automatic response and therefore cannot be sin. Sin is present for sure. Sin is lurking in our hearts before the incident happens and plays a part in the development of anger. Also, there is no question that when we get angry we set ourselves up to do something, or say something, that is sin. It is very important that your group understands this; otherwise they will get the idea that anger is sin and try to deal with it in some way that will cause more problems than the incident in the first place. We will deal with how to handle anger in the coming chapters.

The question dealing with the difference between 4:26 and 4:31 can be resolved by understanding that in 4:36 Paul is talking about the emotion (an automatic response) of anger and stating that it is not a sin. Where sin enters the picture here is in the possible results of the anger. In 4:31 anger is a part of a string and the whole string is rooted in bitterness and therefore simply an outworking of that sinful unwillingness to forgive. Being thus it needs to be put away from you.

By the way, the whole idea of "flared nostrils" is a true Hebrew expression. The Hebrew language does not have words to express some intangible concepts. Therefore, they have to use tangible word pictures to express these intangible concepts. Anger is one of the intangible concepts that is expressed by saying "he flared his nostrils." They do not have the word "have" for example. In order to express "I have" they would say, "there is to me." To say, "he is sad," they would say, "his heart is heavy." There are several other examples, but I think you get the idea.

CHAPTER 3
HOW MAD ARE YOU?

ON MY OWN

Go to the "Pulling It Together" section. Are you beginning to get the rhythm for how to study Jay's book?

1. What is the result of failing to process anger biblically?
2. What are the four possible ways to process anger?
3. What part does your perspective play in controlling anger?

As you can see, this chapter is about processing anger.

1. What, according to Jay, is "chicken-hearted anger"?
2. What are some symptoms of repressed anger?
3. To what was Dr. Brandt referring when he asked, "Would you say the fruit of the Spirit, as defined by Galatians 5:22-23, typifies the way you feel?"
4. How did Dr. Brandt tell Jay to process his anger?

Jay takes an example from Numbers 16. Before you go on, stop, put the book down and turn in your Bible to Numbers 16. Read this chapter before you read the next section of Jay's book. This will give you a background for Jay's comments.

What is the difference in Moses' behavior in verse 4 and 15?

Now go ahead and read the sections entitled "Moses got it off his chest" and "Perspective is the key."

What was the key behavior that changed Jay and Mary's relationship in the last section of this chapter?

DISCUSSION QUESTIONS FOR CHAPTER 3

1. Discuss the consequences that can be observed when a person gets angry and processes it with each of the four methods (expression, suppression, repression, and confession).
2. Discuss the relationship Galatians 5:22-23 have with the processing of anger.
3. If anger is not sin, why was Jay not filled with the Spirit when he was angry with Dr. Brandt?
4. How does one's confidence and self-image affect the aptitude for anger in one's life?

NOTES FOR GROUP LEADERS

Begin your group discussion by talking about the four ways of processing anger. Have each member of the group share his own style of processing anger. Remember the expressers will be the most obvious, but the other styles will be present in your group. The most difficult to identify will be the repressers. They more than likely will not recognize their repression. If your group has a strong relationship with one another you may be able to have each person share about what they see in each other. However, I would encourage you not to get into this type of sharing about one another unless you are sure your group can handle the intimacy.

Be sure to take your group to Numbers 16 and look at Moses and how he handled the rebellion that took place. Point out the difference in the reactions recorded in verse 4 in contrast to verse 15. I would encourage you to make sure you have read, studied and understood the incident in Numbers 16 thoroughly before the group meeting. In fact, you need to back up a few chapters and get a good understanding of the situation that Israel was facing in the wilderness. This incident comes not too long after the fiasco at Kadesh-barnea in Numbers 14.

The story of the encounter with Dr. Brandt is a good place to talk about the relationship of anger to a person's walk with the Lord.

Be sure to emphasize the truth that confession is the correct way of processing anger. Any other process is not only harmful, but it is also sinful.

In the next chapter we are going to talk about forgiveness. This is the logical next step in processing anger. Confession is a necessary first step that must be followed by forgiveness. Also, we are closing in on the first rump-thumping chapter. Start planting seeds now to prepare your group to take action when we get there.

CHAPTER 4
DEALING WITH ANGER BIBLICALLY

ON MY OWN

Check out the "Pulling It Together" section. You will notice that harboring our anger grieves the Holy Spirit and quenches His power. Also, forgiving is a decision and an act of faith, and one does not have to feel like forgiving to do it. Thirdly, forgetting is not necessary. With these three thoughts firmly implanted in our minds let's begin reading.

As you read this chapter look for answers to these questions:

1. What is the cost of hanging on to our anger?
2. What is involved in forgiveness?

DISCUSSION QUESTIONS FOR CHAPTER 4

1. What are the two problems that are faced by someone who is bitter with someone, angry at God, or mad at himself?
2. How do bitterness and the filling of the Spirit relate to one another?

3. What are the two halves of the cost of hanging on to our bitterness?
4. What is the menu at the banquet table of anger?
5. What relationship does feelings have with forgiveness?
6. Relate forgiving someone to:

     Forgetting

     Telling

     Trusting

7. If it impossible to be reconciled to someone, can I ever again experience the filling of the Holy Spirit? Explain your answer.
8. Under what circumstances should you not seek reconciliation? Why not?

NOTES FOR GROUP LEADERS

The first three paragraphs are a series of questions designed to get the reader to focus on his anger and recognize that anger usually falls in one of these three categories. Read over these paragraphs and talk about how members of your group find themselves getting angry. Recognizing our anger and seeing it as a foothold is the first step in dealing with it properly.

The passage that Jay refers to in the next section is Matthew 18:21-35. You may want to read this passage beforehand for your own background, or you may want to use the passage for a discussion starter.

In working through the questions for this chapter lean heavily on these truths:

1. Conscious bitterness and the filling of the Holy Spirit are mutually exclusive.
2. Feeling like forgiving someone and actually forgiving them are two different things. .
3. A "Polar Bear Alert" is the best took to use when trying to forget an offense.

4. Because you forgive someone does not mean that you must now automatically trust that person. Trust is something earned. When it is broken, it must be re-earned, and broken trust is always harder to re-earn than it was to earn it in the first place.

5. Don't bypass the word about not attempting to reconcile in matters of morality or sexual sins. The higher rule on these matters is to flee youthful lusts. There will be more about this in the next group of chapters. Read ahead if you think it necessary.

CHAPTER 5
IT'S TIME TO THUMP THE DEVIL'S RUMP—PART 1

ON MY OWN

This chapter is different. There is no "Pulling It Together" for us to look at first. This is not a chapter to understand, as much is it as a chapter to do. By all means do not skip this chapter. The essence of all Jay has to say is wrapped up in this chapter and the others like it.

Here is how the chapter is structured. First, there is an explanation of how the chapter proceeds; then there is a section on establishing the authority of Christ in this matter; finally there is a series of prayers and statements of resistance. The first prayer is one to establish your position of authority over Satan, which is then followed by resistance. Next are prayers for those of us who are bitter toward someone else, toward God, or toward ourselves. The final prayer is one of thanksgiving. Don't overlook this.

There is a suggestion for you to make a tangible record of what you have done in this chapter. This is an important step and one you should not skip. Stop now and write it down in your Bible before you forget it.

NOTES FOR GROUP LEADERS

In this chapter there is not much to discuss. The point of this chapter is to do something. Rather than talking about this chapter, take the lead and have each member of the group pray through these prayers. It generally works better when each person does this alone. Therefore, I suggest that you begin your session with a few instructions and then send the members to places where they can be alone and insist that each one read through each of the prayers out loud. When they have finished with the prayers and resisting, reassemble and share with each other what went on when they spent time dealing with Satan, using the authority of Christ and His work for us on the cross.

One caution. This chapter presupposes that the reader is a believer in Jesus. Without this foundation there is no basis for claiming authority or expecting anything from God. Make sure that you make this clear. It may be that you have someone in your group who does not know the Lord. Now is the time to deal with the matter of salvation with that person.

Warfare to Break Footholds of Immorality—
Sometimes It's Sin and Sometimes It's Not. . .
or, Will I Burn If I Get the Hots?

We are now moving into the second major division of *Counterattack*. This section deals with immorality as the title suggests. Chapters 6-9 give us the information we need to know, and chapter 10 is another one of those rump-thumping chapters.

CHAPTER 6
WHEN DOES FOOLING AROUND BECOME SIN?

ON MY OWN

Let's start with the "Pulling It Together" section. Make it a point to understand all of these points before you begin reading. This chapter is going to deal with mastery, absolute sin, and variable sin. These are important concepts and must not be confused.

As you read, look for the meaning of "mastery," and look for his development of the concepts of "absolute sin" and "variable sin."

DISCUSSION QUESTIONS FOR CHAPTER 6

1. When does a person outgrow problems with sex?
2. According to statistics, more problems with sex occur among young people. Do you agree with this statement or not? Explain your answer.
3. What is the most often asked question in the Christian world?
4. Explain the concept of "mastery." Give examples of how it works.
5. What constitutes an "absolute sin"?
6. At what point can we say that sexual activity becomes "absolute sin"?
7. What constitutes a variable area of life where an activity may or may not be sinful?
8. How do "Éclairs in Your Refrigerator" affect your performance in the variable areas of life?
9. List some of the principles that will guide you in determining what to do in the variable areas of life.

NOTES FOR GROUP LEADERS

This is a key chapter in dealing with sexual sins, and as you can see by the first paragraph of this chapter, sexual sins are a major problem at every point of our life. We never outgrow it. Spend as much time as necessary to develop the concept of "mastery." This is a key to a successful understanding of proper behavior in this area of our lives. Also, emphasize that when God has spoken specifically about an issue it can no longer be considered a variable. Understanding that they are wrong is not necessary. If God says it is wrong, it is wrong, whether we know about it not. It is only those things about which God has not given specific instructions that can become variables.

Work with your group to develop a strategy for determining how to deal with the variables in their lives. This will be a healthy exercise and will be one that will have continuing impact on their lives.

CHAPTER 7
THE CONSEQUENCES OF SEXUAL SIN

ON MY OWN

Begin with the "Pulling It Together" section. As you read the chapter look for a discussion of the importance of sexual sins. The usual route that entraps most people is compromise, and the outcome of sexual sins is bitterness, memory scars, and the fact that things can never be the same afterward.

You may wonder just where Jay is going as you read this chapter. This is because he has to back up and set a theological stage for his point. Compromise will get you into a sin that seems no worse than any other, but when the dust settles you find your head filled with all sorts of monsters. Jay's theological digression is addressing this point and it is an important one. So, hang in with him, he won't lead you astray.

DISCUSSION QUESTIONS FOR CHAPTER 7

1. When does Beth begin her compromise?
2. Who were the winners in this episode? Who were the losers?
3. Where does our sin nature come from?
4. Why is the virgin birth of Jesus so important?
5. What is the difference between sexual sins and other sins?
6. How do the stories of Noah and Lot describe God's attitude toward sex sins?
7. What mistake did Tamar make in the story from 2 Samuel 13?
8. Describe the monsters that grew out of the story of Amnon and Tamar.
9. Assume that Tamar is your daughter, how would you counsel her?

NOTES FOR GROUP LEADERS

Jay is swimming upstream here. Most of the world sees nothing wrong with sex. To their credit sex is designed by God to fit in its proper place and all of the drives that get us into trouble are also created by God. So with an understanding that sex is good and the drives are God given we must build a case for sexual purity. All this must be done in a context that shouts, "If sex is good let's do it!" You will need to go with your group back into the theological discussion of the sin nature, where it comes from, and how it is transmitted to us. This comes up in the story of Kim and the stereo. Don't gloss over this situation. It is foundational to the argument that sex sins are different and more serious than others.

In this chapter you will want to make sure that you emphasize the dangers of compromise. The section entitled "You Can Stop" is an important one to spend some time with especially if your group contains singles.

When you come to question 9 (on previous page) about counseling your daughter, approach it from two angles. First, how would you counsel her before the incident. Then, how would you counsel her after the incident is over (assume that you did not talk to her beforehand). What would you do if you warned her beforehand and she went ahead against your counsel?

If you want to discuss the story of Amnon and Tamar in context you will find it in 2 Samuel 13.

In the section where Jay talks about Amnon's monster he talks about the bitterness that results from sexual intercourse before marriage. If your group contains married people you may face this situation. In this case, point them to the Appendix and encourage them to follow the instructions there. Don't wait until you get to the end of the book for this appendix. It is important to deal with this monster as soon as possible. And there is no time like the present. If you have a couple that has coupled too son send them away right now to deal with this issue. If you have several couples in your group, why not stop at this point and send them all away with the Appendix and ask them all to read it and follow the instructions whether they need it or not. That way those who need it (even those who don't think they need it but really do) will get it and those who don't need it won't be hurt by it.

CHAPTER 8
CHANGING IMMORAL BEHAVIOR

ON MY OWN

"Pulling It Together" lets us know that this chapter is about God's forgiveness and how we can break bad habits. So let's read, looking for practical help in dealing with sex sins. Jay will tell two stories in this chapter. Both of them are derived from the Gospel of John. The story of Nancy comes from chapter 4 and the other one from chapter 8. You may want to read these stories in the Bible before reading Jay's version of them.

DISCUSSION QUESTIONS FOR CHAPTER 8

1. In the story of Nancy, what were the two elements that came together to form saving faith?
2. In the previous chapter we discussed how sexual sins are different from other sins. That being so, how are sexual sins dealt with by God?
3. In the story of the woman at the temple, what are the two keys to forgiveness?
4. How does the concept of "Éclairs in Your Refrigerator" that we discussed earlier, affect this story?
5. What is the principle for breaking bad habits?
6. Make a list of bad habits that are common and discuss what can be done to apply Jay's principle for breaking bad habits.
7. Summarize the principle in the story of the "Seventy times Seven" story.
8. Read the sentence in italics on page 112. Why is this principle so important?

NOTES FOR GROUP LEADERS

First of all, I would suggest that you read the stories that Jay uses in this chapter in their contexts in the Scriptures. This will give you a background that will be helpful. In fact, you may want to discuss the stories from their biblical context rather than using Jay's paraphrase. If this is easier for you be my guest.

It is important that you stress the concepts of forgiveness for sin. All sins, including sexual sins, are forgiven in Christ. Jay mentions "Éclairs in Your Refrigerator" in this chapter. If you need to refresh your memory of what this word picture is all about, go back to chapter 9. This deals with the important matter of repentance. Remember that repentance involves a change of heart. As long as our heart is turned in the right direction we will be able to deal with our stumbling from time to time.

The section on decreasing your confession time is a crucial one. We all too often give up when we try to do our best and falter. Our natural attitude is "What is the use, I'll never get victory over this. I might as well cash it in and call it quits." This is playing into the enemy's hand. That is just what he wants us to think. If we can grasp the principle that Jay is teaching in this section, we are on the path to ultimate victory over the mastery of a bad habit.

Jay mentions the snake on the stick in Numbers 21. It may become necessary for you to explain the concept there. Read Numbers 21 before you come to the discussion of this chapter so you will be prepared to explain what is meant by this figure. In short, when Israel was in the wilderness they grumbled against God and Moses, and God sent snakes into the camp. Many of the people repented, God instructed Moses to erect a bronze serpent on a stick in the midst of the camp. Whenever anyone was bitten they could simply look at the bronze serpent and be cured. Those who chose not to look at the bronze serpent died of snakebite.

CHAPTER 9
GOD'S SOLUTION TO SEXUAL TEMPTATION

ON MY OWN

"Pulling It Together" tips us off that this chapter is about God's strategy for dealing with sexual temptation, about being trusted with sexual temptation, and about policing ourselves. It is a short chapter mainly because God's strategy is simple and straightforward. Whenever you encounter sexual temptation, run.

DISCUSSION QUESTIONS FOR CHAPTER 9

1. In the story about the lady with the luggage in the motel parking lot, when did Jay make his decision? What are other possible times he could have made his decision, and what would have been the consequences of each?
2. How long does a person need to demonstrate consistent trustworthiness before he can be trusted in matters of sexual temptation?
3. Discuss the principles involved in the story about Kim and her boyfriend.
4. When are you most vulnerable to sexual temptation?
5. Discuss the problems and solutions involved in counseling or praying with a member of the opposite sex.
6. What are the dangers involved in hugging and giving back rubs?

NOTES FOR GROUP LEADERS

This is a short but important chapter. You might want to include the story of Joseph in Genesis 39 in your discussion of this chapter. Here is a Bible story of a young man faced with a strong sexual temptation and how he dealt with it. We cannot emphasize enough the need to put distance between yourself and sexual temptation. Use as many situations as you can to illustrate the point. In the story about Jay in the motel, the intent of the question is to locate as many decision points as possible and ascertain the consequences of each. There are more conservative decision points and there are obviously points of decision that are more dangerous. Try to look at the positive and negative aspects of each.

The "Are You Playing With Fire" section is an important one especially if you are dealing with a group of married persons. If you have couples in your group this may be a little awkward but don't skip this section. Couples need to deal with temptation well before it gets dangerous. Suggest that the couples discuss these questions on their own as a couple. In fact, if your group is all couples, send them away during the session to discuss it now. If you have a mixed group, I would still send the couples off by themselves to talk about this matter. If you are dealing with married guys only or married women only, take the time in the group to discuss these questions. If your group has developed a critical level of intimacy they may be able to share struggles and difficulties with the group. If so, then you can hold one another accountable.

In the matter of holding one another accountable, encourage spouses to be accountable to one another. Perceptive wives can be life savers for their husbands when they get cornered by someone in a dangerous situation. Ladies, never forget that you will see a temptation coming well before your husband sees it. Do whatever you can to get between him and the temptation. That may mean doing something uncomfortable for you and make you look foolish or like a jealous wife. No matter, your home is worth it, take my word.

CHAPTER 10
IT'S TIME TO THUMP THE DEVIL'S RUMP—PART 2

ON MY OWN

This chapter, like chapter 5, is an action chapter. There is no new information in this chapter, just instructions for what needs to be done with the information for the last four chapters.

Don't skip this chapter! Read it carefully and do what Jay asks you to do in it.

The format is this: As you read, Jay will give you instructions on what to do at each step of the way. Read the instructions, pray the prayers and resist at the appropriate times. Take note that Jay emphasizes the need for patience in this chapter, so don't rush through it. Also, there is the suggestion to look back at chapter 5 to refresh your mind of the authority you have in Christ.

Take your time, when you are finished we will dive into chapter 11.

NOTES FOR GROUP LEADERS

Just like in chapter 5 we will have to resist the strong temptation to skip this chapter and move on into the new subject matter. Take it from me, resist the temptation and spend the time necessary for this chapter. There is no greater need for people than to get the garbage out of their lives and begin to live a life of purity before God.

You will face the temptation to become the "tour guide" for this exercise. Resist this temptation also. You need to be clean before the Lord even more than your group does. Here is my suggestion: Work through the chapter before the group meeting. That way you will be clean going in. Then as you lead the group through the exercise it will be familiar ground. Resist the temptation to jump out of the activity and just be an instructor for the group members even though you have already gone through the exercise. Your role as a model for your group is an important role for you to play. They will be watching you and they need to see in you a sincerity and an intensity that matches the seriousness of this subject.

Take time with this chapter and be patient with your group. Give them plenty of time to deal with each of the elements. You may want to give instructions to them and send them off to pray and rebuke out loud as Jay suggests. In this case, you may be calling them together and sending them out several times during the course of the session. Another alternative is to give instructions and have them stay in the room and deal with each of the matters silently. This will avoid all of the moving around. It makes no difference what you choose. You make the choice for your group.

After you have completed the exercises in this chapter bring the group together to share. By now you will have been together as a group for 10 sessions and should have developed some intimacy with one another. This should be a basis for sharing some intimate things with one another. However, don't force it. If the sharing does not flow freely that's fine. But you need to provide platforms for sharing to take place when it does become natural.

CHAPTER 11
THE COST OF WRONG PRIORITIES

ON MY OWN

Just reading through the "Pulling It Together" section sets us up to look for a chapter dealing with priorities, values and contentment.

DISCUSSION QUESTIONS FOR CHAPTER 11

1. How would you justify your actions if you were Esau? Where was the error in his thinking?
2. Define the terms "vanity of vanities" and "chasing after wind."
3. What is the thing on top of your cone? (Do you want to find out what is on top of your cone? Check the Notes For Group Leaders below for an exercise to determine what is on top of your cone.)
4. In the story of the rich young ruler, what is Jesus saying about money?
5. I thought goals were a good thing. How can they be "wind"?
6. Describe the difference between happiness and contentment.
7. What makes the scene described on pages 136-138 a scene in hell rather than a scene in heaven?
8. How does the situation related by Jay on pages 136-138 relate to Psalm 37:4?

NOTES FOR GROUP LEADERS

A good exercise to help people determine their priorities is to have them choose the 10 most important people or things in their life. (You could use a burning building scenario, or something of the like to establish the limit. Serendipity suggests a game where each player has a given amount of money and then a list of items are auctioned off to the highest bidder. You may have some other creative way to get people to pare down what is important to them. If you have a good one, use it.) Continue the game by moving them to a place where they can only have 8 items, then to 6, to 4 and so on until they have gotten rid of everything but one. What they have left is what they treasure most. This is the thing/person on top of their cone, if it's more important than Christ.

Philippians 4 is the key passage dealing with contentment. Don't quit until your group understands that contentment is not measured by the amount or the quality of what you have, but in your commitment to Christ.

You can have a lively discussion sorting out how money and goals can be both good and bad. Remember that God does not put a premium on poverty or a spontaneous lack of goals. Work with your group to help them understand the proper place of money and goals in their priorities.

The story of the gambler is an enigma. I am not sure that it gives a very clear picture of what hell is like. What it does do is point out that the satisfaction of all of our wants is not satisfying. Some have described hell as a place where raw sin nature is turned loose without restriction. The selfishness that we wrestle with here on earth will find its ultimate expression in hell. I am not sure that is what hell is all about, but it is an interesting thought. C. S. Lewis promotes this idea in his book *The Great Divorce*.

Question 8 (on facing page) is offered to stimulate your discussion about the fulfillment of desires. Getting the desires of one's heart is dependent upon truly delighting yourself in the Lord and not in the desires of the heart. It would seem that getting the desires of your heart is a good and satisfying thing in Psalm 37:4, but Jay seems to picture getting all the desires of your heart as not being satisfying. I leave it to you to work out the difference between the two.

Some Scripture passages that you may need to look at are Genesis 25:29-34, which is the story of Jacob and Esau and the selling of the birthright for a pot of stew, and Luke 18:18-27, which is the story of the rich young ruler.

CHAPTER 12
HOW TO ADJUST YOUR PRIORITIES

ON MY OWN

The "Pulling It Together" section reminds us of polar bear alerts, the slavery principle, and the need to keep a close watch on the éclairs in our refrigerators. When we thumb the chapter we notice one box and several quotes from the Old Testament book of Ecclesiastes. It looks like Jay is going to lead us through a tour of King Solomon's thinking process, and to his conclusion. Certainly the conclusion of the wisest man will have some meaning for us as well.

DISCUSSION QUESTIONS FOR CHAPTER 12

1. Put the concepts "vanity" and "striving after wind" in your own words.
2. Make a list of the things that King Solomon tried in his quest for satisfaction.
3. After his long search, what was Solomon's conclusion?
4. Having looked despair in the face, where did Solomon turn for answers?

NOTES FOR GROUP LEADERS

This chapter mainly deals with an exegesis of Ecclesiastes. Walk your group through the passages in Ecclesiastes and discuss each of the elements that Solomon tried, noting how it falls short of delivering satisfaction. Lead them to the same despair that Solomon felt before opening up the real solution, that is turn to God. It is important to see the complete failure of the world system to produce real satisfaction before we introduce the real answer to man's need. To offer God to people who have not come to the place where they fully understand the bankruptcy of everything else is to produce a shallow commitment. What we need to understand is that we are utterly helpless and hopeless without God's intervention in our lives.

CHAPTER 13
IT'S TIME TO THUMP THE DEVIL'S RUMP—PART 3

ON MY OWN

We have the routine down by now. You will notice this chapter begins with a story that is adapted from Acts 5:1-11. It deals with your heart condition. After you have read the story, continue following Jay's instructions and pray the prayers out loud as you go.

NOTES FOR GROUP LEADERS

What more can I say? You know how to lead your group through this chapter. It is just like chapter 5 and chapter 10. Go for it!

CHAPTER 14
DEBRIEFING: FIX YOUR PENCIL,
MAINTAIN YOUR MENISCUS

ON MY OWN

This is a different kind of a chapter. You probably have already noticed that there is no "Pulling It Together" section at the end of this chapter. What Jay is going to do in this chapter is to talk to you about being filled with the Holy Spirit. He uses the word "meniscus." This may be a new term for you. If so, read the paragraph beginning with "Water has a surface tension." This is where he explains what meniscus means.

Jay mentions seeking some outside counsel. Your pastor is the best source for this. If you don't have a church that you are regularly attending, start looking for one now.

One more time, let's dive into chapter 14. Here are some discussion questions.

DISCUSSION QUESTIONS FOR CHAPTER 14

1. What is the point of the broken pencil illustration?
2. What are the facilitators of repair for our broken pencil? Which is the major facilitator? When will our pencil be fully restored?
3. What does "meniscus" mean and how does it relate to the filling of the Holy Spirit?
4. What is the solution to water being sloshed out of our lives?
5. Why is it not OK to be almost full?
6. What is the mark of a spiritual person?
7. What causes footholds in my life?
8. Explain in your own words what Jay means by the illustration of putting the two-year-old to bed.
9. When is it safe to go into the swamp?

NOTES FOR GROUP LEADERS

In this chapter we are dealing with three important topics: Original sin, filling with the Holy Spirit, and victorious Christian living. It is important for us to understand all three of these doctrines. Understanding that we are held accountable for our sin nature is foundational to our salvation. We are born sinners and only the blood of Jesus can cleanse us from that stain. We are perfect in Christ, but we still walk in a crooked world and wrestle with an active sin nature that is vulnerable to attack from the enemy. Therefore, the broken pencil illustration is vital for us to understand that we are not perfect in our walk (but not to worry, because the blood of Christ has already solved this problem), and that is OK. All is not lost if I mess up.

The doctrine of the filling with the Holy Spirit is what is behind the illustration of the meniscus on the water glass. Spend whatever time necessary for your group to grasp the concept of God looking at our lives from a different vantage point and any unconfessed sin in our lives disqualifies us from being filled with the Holy Spirit.

Stress the importance of increasing the time between sloshings and decreasing the time between sloshing and 1 John 1:9. This is the essence of living the spirit-filled life. Jay mentions it only briefly, but the idea of the steady stream of water being poured into the glass is a closer picture of the Greek meaning of Ephesians 5:18. The word used there literally means "be constantly being filled" with the Holy Spirit. So, you can see that the idea of living in a continual state of confession and repentance is what Paul is commanding. (Yes, commanding. The word is in the imperative mood, which means that it is a command. The implications of this fact are: There are no options, we must be filled with the Holy Spirit, and it is a sin not to be filled with the Holy Spirit.)

Here is a suggestion. Pass out paper and have each person write down these four incomplete sentences. Then give them time to complete them in your group meeting.

1. What I liked most about this study was . . .

2. The most difficult session for me was . . .
3. The decisions I made are . . .
4. What I am struggling with now is . . .

Collect the responses and use them for your own evaluation and follow-up.

OTHER BOOKS BY JAY CARTY

Coach Wooden One-on-One (Regal Books, 2003)—a 60-day devotional with the legendary basketball coach John Wooden.

Coach Wooden's Pyramid of Success: Building Blocks for a Better Life (Regal Books, 2005)—a devotional using coach John Wooden's time-tested philosophy of life.

Darrell Waltrip One-on-One (Regal Books, 2004)—a 60-day devotional with the legendary race car driver and voice of NASCAR on Fox Sports Darrell Waltrip.

Discovering Your Natural Talents: How to Love What You Do and Do What You Love (NavPress, 1994)—a guide to help you find your niche in life and ministry.

O. Whillikers in the Hall of Champions (Regal Books, 2000)—for children ages 7 to 11 who live in single-parent homes or other "at-risk" environments.

Playing with Fire: Do Nice People Really Go to Hell? (Multnomah Publishers, 1992)—a contemporary approach to salvation and apologetics.

Something's Fishy: Getting Rid of the Carp in Your Life (Multnomah Publishers, 1990)—a discussion of the dangers of being lukewarm in your faith.

Please visit my website, www.jaycarty.com, for further information.

Let Jay Carty Introduce You to Lives of Faith

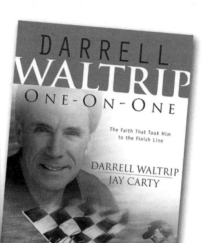

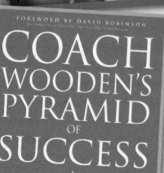

Coach Wooden: One-on-One
Inspiring Conversations on Purpose,
Passion and the Pursuit of Success
John Wooden and *Jay Carty*
ISBN 08307.32918

Darrell Waltrip: One-on-One
The Faith That Took Him to the Finish Line
Darrell Waltrip and *Jay Carty*
ISBN 08307.34635

Coach Wooden's Pyramid of Success
Building Blocks for a Better Life
John Wooden and *Jay Carty*
ISBN 08307.36794

More Great Resources
from Regal Books

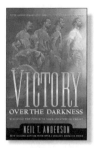

**Victory over
the Darkness**
Realizing the Power of
Your Identity in Christ
Neil T. Anderson
ISBN 08307.25644

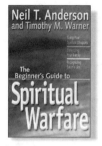

**The Beginner's Guide
to Spiritual Warfare**
Using Your Spiritual
Weapons–Keeping
Spiritually Fit for Battle
*Neil T. Anderson
and Timothy M. Warner*
ISBN 08307.33876

**A Woman's Guide to
Spiritual Warfare**
Quin Sherrer
and *Ruthanne Garlock*
ISBN 08307.35186

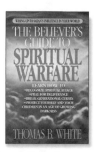

**The Believer's Guide
to Spiritual Warfare**
Wising Up to Satan's
Influence in Your World
Thomas B. White
ISBN 08307.33906

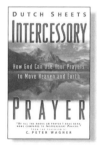

Intercessory Prayer
How God Can Use Your Prayers
to Move Heaven and Earth
Dutch Sheets
ISBN 08307.19008

**Spiritual
Housecleaning**
Protect Your Home and Family
from Spiritual Pollution
Alice and Eddie Smith
ISBN 08307.31075